Praise for J. Michael Coffey and *G.A.L.E. Force*

"Mike Coffey is a unique leader who seamlessly blends a rigor of operational expertise with an innate ability to connect with people within an organization to build and align teams with a mission-focused culture. I had the privilege from the board level to see Mike's skill sets as a CEO, and to observe him build global strategies within a highly matrixed organization that resonated all the way to the teams on the factory floors."

—Steve Tober

CEO, Perspectus, Inc.; former Board Director, Manitex International

"*G.A.L.E. Force* is an extremely well-grounded presentation of the challenges of building, leading, and selling a global manufacturing company. The book is authored by someone who has done it successfully several times. Mike Coffey develops a compelling formula for balancing global economics, local cultural norms, and best implementation practices into an integrated strategy. I highly recommend it."

—Robert K. Kazanjian

Asa Griggs Candler Professor of Organization and Management, Goizueta Business School/Emory University

"The *G.A.L.E. Force* framework is intuitive and useful because it is born of Mike's experience as a leader across geographies and cultures. He refutes centrally controlled business models in favor of local execution, while retaining a common vision for the success of the enterprise."

—Jim Recer
Former Chief Banking Officer

"*G.A.L.E. Force* provides numerous useful insights to the fast-changing M&A world. I have known Michael Coffey for over thirty years and know, for a fact, that he is a credible and well-seasoned expert on strategy, culture, and value creation."

—Charles Snyder
President & Managing Member, C2 Advisory Group LLC

"Mike Coffey is one of those rare people you simply love to be around. I do. His presence fills any room—not because he's boisterous, but because of his strong character and other-focused love. Behind his easy warmth lies a remarkably strategic mind, capable of multiplying business impact on a global scale. Wise, fun, and deeply passionate about people, Mike knows how to scale up relationally coherent businesses that thrive across cultures.

G.A.L.E. Force serves as a guide to help you cultivate the same coherence, resilience, clarity, and vitality that define his approach to leadership and life."

—Dr. Tom Wood
CEO, Gospel Coaching Network; Coauthor of Gospel Coach

G.A.L.E.
Force

NAVIGATING STRATEGY, CULTURE, AND VALUE CREATION IN MODERN M&A

GALE Force

J. MICHAEL COFFEY

Entrepreneur | Books

Published by Entrepreneur® Books, Charleston, South Carolina.
An imprint of Advantage Media Group.

Printed in the United States of America.

10 9 8 7 6 5 4 3 2 1

ISBN: 979-8-89701-069-1 (Paperback)
ISBN: 979-8-89701-070-7 (eBook)

Library of Congress Control Number: 2026906589

Cover design by Lance Buckley.
Layout design by Matthew Morse.

Since 1977, Entrepreneur Media has been dedicated to inspiring, informing, and celebrating the innovators who drive business forward. Entrepreneur® Books, launched in 2024 through a partnership with Entrepreneur Media, continues that mission by helping business and thought leaders share their insights, experiences, and expertise through custom books. Opinions expressed by authors of Entrepreneur® Books are their own. To be considered for publication, please visit books.Entrepreneur.com.

03-26-2026 11:50

To Sherrie, Zoe, and Joelle,

the women in my life who have inspired me to become a better person and have given me my most meaningful roles: husband and father.

CONTENTS

INTRODUCTION

It was 2018, and the country of Chile was riding a wave of optimism. Pope Francis had opened the year with a historic visit, capturing the world's attention. A reform movement offered great promise to working men and women. Government austerity measures were finally reining in runaway inflation. And a copper mining boom, driven by the world's transition to electric, was footing the bill for much of Chile's newfound prosperity. Yet beneath bold headlines of progress, Chile's state-owned mining giant, Codelco, found itself backed up against a hole in the ground—literally.

Years earlier, Codelco had invested in a fleet of Komatsu ultra-class haul trucks to literally move mountains of ore for processing. These electric drive trucks had cost Codelco $5.5 million apiece and were beasts of machines—weighing in at 625 metric tons, boasting thirteen-foot-tall tires, capable of carrying the same weight as a fully loaded Boeing 747. But now these beasts wouldn't be able to deliver for Codelco in its northernmost mine because that mine was tapped out at the surface, and the company needed to move to underground mining. The trucks weren't built for underground.

At the same time, Codelco was undertaking a $1 billion expansion of its Rajo Inca (Salvador) mine to feed the world's appetite for copper. That would require a huge capital expenditure for new Komatsu trucks, unless the company could refurbish its current fleet being used in the south of the country. Refurbishing ultraclass trucks to make them reliable over time was also an expensive proposition for Codelco. They could spend $50 million on such a contract.

Codelco chose to go the refurbishing route. As the original equipment manufacturer (OEM) for the trucks, Komatsu had to be the favored vendor for this refurbishing. They led off the contract bidding, and among the lesser bidders was an outfit named H-E Parts International, with its Chilean general manager, Alfonso Teplizky, pushing to win what would be the company's largest order.

Beating Komatsu on scale and resources would have been near impossible, since Komatsu had the OEM advantage and had invested billions in the market. But Alfonso was also there on the ground with the Codelco team; he had been general manager of Morgan Chile, which H-E Parts had previously acquired, and was keenly tied in to the local mining culture and its needs. So instead of offering the same solutions as other vendors might, Alfonso's H-E Parts bid focused on innovative, tailored solutions. Instead of restoring the big trucks to their original condition, H-E Parts offered to incorporate quality enhancements that had proven out in Australia and North America, while also preparing the trucks for relocation and thus satisfying the RFP, adding additional value.

Alfonso believed that if H-E Parts' bid price was close enough, if the solution was innovative enough to get the trucks back to work fast, and if the local H-E Parts team could be flexible to the needs of the local miners rather than beholden to the far-off Japanese conglomerate Komatsu, H-E Parts might stand a chance.

He was right.

Little H-E Parts Thumps the Goliath Komatsu

As CEO of H-E Parts at the time, I was intensely proud of our Chilean operation for winning the contract. But I was even prouder of how precisely it validated our commitment to a "global ambition, local execution" strategy.

That strategy on that day elevated H-E Parts in Chile from that of a small distributor to a slightly larger provider of *innovative* equipment refurbishing solutions. Until this point, our largest on-site contract in Chile was the operation of a truck-cleaning operation, essentially a labor agreement to operate a truck wash.

Innovation was the crucial bit.

When Codelco was faced with the daunting challenge of rehabbing twenty-four haul trucks to give them extended operating life, they figured the cost at $6 million a pop—a substantial investment of $140 million in all, along with a lot of downtime. But our engineering teams figured out a minimum set of fixes that could be completed for $2.3 million or so apiece to give those big trucks another sixty-thousand-plus hours of use. In addition, by design, we would coordinate refurbishment to mitigate customer downtime.

Ultimately, Codelco awarded the contract to three contractors for security reasons. H-E Parts received and completed the bulk of the refurbishments. It was a big win for us. And it was a testament to a management approach and mergers and acquisitions (M&A) buildup strategy we'd begun just five years prior.

As management approaches go, our decision had been a case study in getting the strategy right and executing in a decentralized and effective manner. We could have pursued the traditional global strategy that many industrial organizations follow—imposing our talents on the world at large. We could have gone the multidomestic way—granting wide independence and autonomy to our local operations at our thirty-five facilities in seven countries. But we chose something of a hybrid approach—developing a global infrastructure that supported and brought out the best in our local implementation teams.

Developing Strategy for the Lower-Middle Markets

This hybrid approach can be described as ***Global Aim, Local Execution***—or, as we shorthand it, the **G.A.L.E. Force Strategy** that trims the company sails to harness local winds into a global accelerant!

It works because companies do not cross the oceans of commerce by drifting or by brute force. They advance by setting a clear bearing and then capturing the strongest winds already moving in that direction—winds created by local market dynamics, regulatory realities, customer expectations, and cultural nuances. The skill lies in reading those gusts early, adjusting the rigging continuously, and riding the pressure rather than resisting it. With the right navigation, what would otherwise be destabilizing crosswinds become the very forces that drive speed, momentum, and reach—even drive them with gale-force tenacity … which is the **G.A.L.E. Force** in action.

Our success at using this strategy at H-E Parts to enter seven countries, acquire fourteen entities, and assemble them into a global platform was ultimately validated when H-E Parts itself was acquired by Hitachi Construction Machinery (HCM) for $240 million in 2016.

Our founder, JP Richard, was to M&A buildups what Ahab was to his whale—impossibly driven. Or what Elon Musk has been to moonshots—irrepressibly optimistic. Nothing was going to stop this brilliant Stanford scholar from acquiring and acquiring until H-E Parts was the largest independent provider of aftermarket parts, components, and remanufacturing services for the mining, construction, and energy industries. With a senior team of Steve McBrayer, Ian Olivieri, and me, H-E Parts became a strategic acquisition juggernaut in these sectors.

JP entered every room, it seemed, with his hand extended and ready to shake on a deal. Every business owner he met in our sector was given an offer, sometimes right there on the spot, punctuated by his favorite promise: "H-E Parts is going to buy your business, and nothing will change, nothing!" Words I must have heard dozens of times. And JP meant them. In his mind, nothing would change after a deal was inked.

And that's where Steve, Ian, and I came in. We'd have lunch with an entrepreneur who, in most cases, had never sold a company before. Never endured the gauntlet of vetting, due diligence, negotiations, integration. They'd be nervous, uncertain, wondering what would happen next. But JP had been at this table dozens of times, as had the rest of our team. In our minds, we wanted the entrepreneur's success to continue. We loved that success. After all, that success was why we were there in the first place. And there was always a temptation to not change a thing. We want the business to keep thriving, after all.

But the reality is, everything changes when companies merge—and for all the right reasons. How could it be otherwise? Whether a company has been around for thirty years, fifteen, or five, it can't help but change when it begins working side by side with another enterprise.

One of the misunderstandings in M&A comes from the cultural myths we grew up with. Many of today's entrepreneurs were raised on films such as *Wall Street* and *Pretty Woman*, where ruthless corporate raiders tore apart the companies they bought and seemed to revel in the wreckage. Those stories taught a generation to fear mergers, to consider them vile acts of destruction. But they *were* dramas, those films and others like them. Meant solely to entertain and reflect reality only as much as drama requires.

In truth, the M&A world is more nuanced and constructive than Hollywood ever lets on.

In real life, some companies are acquired and left intact, continuing to generate profits with little disruption. Others experience gradual change at first and then transformation over time—usually for the better. That's the norm, a healthy norm.

Change Should Be the Constant in M&A

When a company is acquired, there can't help but be a passel of changes, and whether they are good or bad depends on how well the deal was crafted. As for the common changes:

- Every employee who stays on gains a new set of leaders, reporting lines, and expectations.
- There's a new bank involved, new finance and accounting standards, and new investor priorities.
- New IT systems must be integrated, vendor contracts renegotiated, and HR policies and benefit plans aligned.
- Marketing teams rebrand, sales teams learn new incentive structures, and compliance departments adjust to new jurisdictions.
- Culture begins to recalibrate right down to how decisions, big and little, get made as two sets of habits and histories are woven together.

And then comes the most demanding phase of all. Figuring out how to leverage the whole point of the acquisition. To extract the synergies everyone hoped for? To expand market capabilities while preparing the business to scale? To resize the workforce?

Reaching full agreement between the acquired team and the new parent company is not unlike herding cats who each think they own the barn, or merging two families who both insist Thanksgiving be at their house every year.

Even when both companies' strategies are in alignment—as they often are in good acquisitions—the way strategy has been executed is rarely a mirror image.

The reality is that an entrepreneur selling their business in a merger has to be, and should want to be, ready for change. Because those changes, when managed well, are what make the acquisition successful—and justify the multiple that was paid. Justifying it well and rewarding handsomely.

CHANGE IS NOT JUST THE SELLER'S BURDEN

This became strikingly clear on my first visit to Santiago, Chile, a few years before the Komatsu big truck deal took place. H-E Parts had a nascent track record as a global enterprise, and I was inexperienced with Chilean ways. We had recently acquired Morgan and Crown Parts Machinery, and I was excited about how we, as a still small American equipment parts company, could make a difference in the mining businesses in Chile.

I had carefully scheduled a weeklong itinerary with our teams in Chile that would cap off with a high-profile meeting with one of our best customers—the largest mine in Chile, BHP's Escondida. I arrived on a Sunday in June for a full agenda—ready to talk about our expansion plans and prepare for the BHP Escondida meeting. It was winter in Chile, and cold, but I was warm with optimism. At least until we arrived for our meeting to find our customer's offices nearly empty and our key customer contacts absent. Now I was feeling really frosty. What was going on?

Between scheduling the trip and the week of, the Chilean national team had advanced to play Peru in a high-stakes semifinal of the Copa América. It was 2015, and Chile had a real chance at its first title, which it eventually won in July against Argentina. Essentially, the whole of Chile was on furlough to watch their team play a regional rival. It was an unscheduled holiday, and my plans would have to wait. I had never seen a city, let alone a country, shut down for a sporting event.

No one at the office had the heart to disappoint me with this news. To my team and our customer, watching their national team in the semifinals was the obvious thing to be doing. I spent that day in a hotel room learning a valuable lesson. I had come to change a local culture to my managerial liking, and I didn't even understand the culture I meant to change.

So how could I possibly change it?

And why should I?

These two questions would inform my thinking for the rest of the visit when the crew returned to the office, and we got down to planning our business future together.

This planning crystallized our team's thinking about how a global operation like ours could localize at scale and, in four years' time, double the size of a business that had been growing in the high single digits, going from $18 million to $53 million in sales. All from dedicating to a strategy, and then executing on it.

Our work—then and now—could not have been unfolding at a better moment. Across industries, a new wave of M&A expansion has been gathering steam. Both buyers and sellers of companies—especially in the lower-middle market—have become something of the belle of a ballroom brimming with high-stakes takeovers and big-money exits. And great fortunes are being made by those who understand how the game is played now.

So let's widen the lens. Let's look at how swiftly the M&A world is changing—and what that means for all of us who live and thrive in it.

Strongest Forces Blowing Across the World Today

Right now, four enormous forces are sweeping across the global business landscape. They aren't gentle breezes—they're jet streams. They're moving capital at historic speed, reshaping companies in every sector, and rewriting long-standing assumptions about ownership and control. In sheer scale and impact, this moment rivals the economic explosions that followed World War II.

Before we talk about how to handle these forces, it helps to understand what they are and why they matter. So let's take a quick tour through each one. Let's see how they are coming together to create some of the biggest opportunities business owners and investors have seen in a generation.

RETIRING BUSINESS OWNERS PUT A LOT OF INVESTMENTS INTO PLAY

There are about 320,000 businesses in just the territorial United States with annual sales of $5 to $100 million. Most of these businesses are owned by Boomers—seven in ten of whom will have to hand over the reins in the coming decade, whether they like it or not, based solely on their advancing age.

When we focus solely on US businesses that may go onto the market as acquisition targets in the coming decade, we rely on data from DealStream and other sources to identify some 7,400 industrial businesses with \$5–\$100 million in sales where (a) the owner will soon be aging out and retiring and (b) there is uncertainty about the line of succession and what will happen next.

In most cases, these owners' children won't be taking over the family business. There is a myriad of data on this subject, and it varies widely. One study indicates that only a minority of businesses will successfully transition within the family. Another shows a majority will. As for what's most likely to happen, I suspect that PwC's analysts have the strongest insights. They believe that 41 percent of family-owned businesses will be handed over to the next generation, 11 percent will pass the ownership to family but not the management reins, and 30 percent will sell to a third party. If this is close to accurate, it presents a lot of opportunity for investors.

Which is why, the second force …

LOWER-MIDDLE MARKET DEALS ARE PROVING FRUITFUL

While megadeals often dominate headlines, it's the midmarket and smaller transactions that have been yielding stronger returns with lower risks, as well. McKinsey's analysis of Global 1,000 M&A activity from 1999 to 2010 and again from 2007 to 2017 revealed that companies engaging in moderately sized M&A deals regularly outperform those that don't, delivering superior shareholder returns over the long term.

This suggests that dealmakers are increasingly favoring smaller, more manageable transactions. The appeal of smaller and lower-middle market deals is clear: They are less susceptible to global economic fluctuations, face fewer regulatory hurdles, and require less capital, all of which reduces shareholder anxiety. This environment is particularly advantageous as well for Baby Boomer entrepreneurs seeking exit strategies that align with their values and future aspirations.

An equally critical factor for many smaller companies is the requirement of scale simply to remain alive. In many industries—especially tech, media, healthcare, and energy—scale isn't a stop on the road map but a must-have. A combination of factors—principally digital transformation, platform dominance, the network effects imperative, and skyrocketing R&D costs—makes it far more efficient to merge than to try to go it alone.

The so-called urge to merge is accelerating across almost every sector, based on what we are seeing. It is drawing in many players who see opportunities in buildup strategies that create a powerful platform in a given vertical (which we'll talk a lot more about).

And of course, this consolidation activity is drawing the most attention from the big asset players on Wall Street and beyond who are applying a top-down force on today's M&A dynamic.

BIG ASSET PLAYERS SEE A VIRTUOUS CYCLE

Private equity and sovereign wealth funds are not just active—they are awash in capital and needing to deploy it. The so-called dry powder held on private equity balance sheets in 2025 totaled roughly $1.2 trillion. An estimated 25 percent of this capital has been held on the books for four-plus years, increasing the pressure on dealmakers to do the job they're paid to do—find quality deals and close them.

Then there's the world's sovereign wealth funds bringing even greater firepower to the acquisition hunt. These funds now command assets estimated in the $13–$14 trillion range, and a number of them are explicitly seeking higher yield and direct investments.

The future is always uncertain, but as I write in late 2025, the private-equity (P/E) industry appears to have awakened from a long hibernation and is gearing up for dealmaking. P/E insiders are betting that (a) a global appetite for lowering interest rates, (b) deeper rounds of tax cuts ahead, and (c) a loosening of regulatory roadblocks worldwide, along with (d) the AI wild card, are going to act like a powerful spur in the rear end of buyers and sellers.

Top execs at big-name asset players such as Ares Management, Blackstone, and KKR are reporting a 2.5-times bump in NDAs signed (which generally precedes increased deal flow) as well as the possible start of a virtuous cycle of transactions ahead. And they're putting hundreds of billions where their mouth is.

Money is, in short, flowing freely.

Supporting this bullishness by big-name players is the actual activity we're seeing. In the first half of 2025, P/E-sponsored exits totaled $308 billion across 215 transactions. That's the best first half in three years—in terms of both deal speed and scale. If the cycle continues this robustly, it should spin out all kinds of opportunities for, as well as put intense pressures on, M&A activity in the small business markets.

This pressure is likely to intensify as strategic buyers compete not only with one another but also with the big-name asset players who can offer aggressive pricing and creative financing structures. These big players hold some $1.3 trillion in capital ready to invest and own about 10,000 companies worth as much as $4 trillion, insiders at Morgan Stanley say. So they are looking for the right reasons to pull the trigger.

Having the right strategy at hand to take advantage of these first three opportunities (great numbers of retiring business owners, lower-middle market deals proving fruitful, big asset players seeing a virtuous cycle ahead) is the ante for any serious player in today's multicultural world. It also sets up the fourth and perhaps most critical force driving M&A …

AN M&A STRATEGY FOR MAXIMIZING GLOBAL BUSINESS EXCELLENCE

For much of the twentieth century, business leaders were impressed by and tried to emulate the "Welch management system," a.k.a. "GE's operating system." GE CEO Jack Welch aimed to lock in a single, consistent management and performance system across every GE office, wherever it may be. But the world Welch operated within has come and gone.

Events and technologies in the 1970s began tearing down the old nationalist precepts that had both informed and constrained business, and a new sense of the world marketplace started to take shape. We were not becoming "one world" as so many naively predicted. Instead, we were seeing a thousand local cultures blossom with an unexpected fervor (we just didn't know it yet).

When some of the sharpest analysts began surveying this phenomenon in the late 1980s, they coalesced around a new idea of "globalization rising." First to write authoritatively on the subject was McKinsey Managing Director Kenichi Ohmae. In his 1990 business bestseller *The Borderless World*, Ohmae took on the old ways of business …

> *"It is hard to let old beliefs go … Like a man who has worn eyeglasses so long … we forget that the world looks to us the way*

it does because we have become used to seeing it that way … Today, however, we need new lenses. And we need to throw the old ones away."

It was prescient thinking as world markets were in fact becoming much more interlinked, and multinational companies needed to figure out and adapt to local tastes, beliefs, and behaviors. In Ohmae's view back then …

"Contemporary global corporations have to serve the needs of customer segments. Instead of educating the 'barbarians' to drink coke or eat cornflakes, they have to discover the basic drinking and eating needs of people and serve these needs."

This was about as deep as Ohmae and his similarly visionary peers went. In reading his words today, one might detect a hegemonic view of the world's markets, a paternalist streak that ran top-down through the day's management nostrums. Ohmae and his similarly visionary peers shared a pressing agenda—the normalization of "globalization and efficiency." To such a way of thinking, a multinational that sought to enter a new global market only to run headlong into local differences ought to remedy the situation by being accommodating when possible but overriding when necessary … rather than supporting local cultural values for their own sake.

An Ohmae peer, British sociologist Roland Robertson, characterized this new business outlook as "glocalization" and subsequently defined it in his 1992 book *Globalization: Social Theory and Global Culture.* But Robertson was still talking about "adapting" global strategies to local conditions, implying quite the top-down approach.

Such an approach undoubtedly appealed to those sitting atop the world's business pyramids, but not so much to those on the bottom … who were becoming increasingly empowered as we entered a new millennium. For as it turned out, perhaps paradoxically to the thought leaders of the time, the more connected the world became, the more local cultures began celebrating and even insisting on their differentness.

Companies with offices in ten countries began finding that they might have ten different interpretations and executions of their strategic vision. Even if these executions were only different in nuanced ways, they were crucially driven by the local cultural requirements of all the company's stakeholders. This meant that company managers had to migrate fully from culture-blindness to culture-mindedness. For many, this was no small lift.

The Fast-Evolving Nature of the M&A Deal

In looking at these four forces—a generation massively retiring, lower market deals proving the most fruitful, big asset players seeing a virtuous M&A cycle, and the cultural imperative of a "global aim, local execution" strategy—we see a lot of unpreparedness in today's executive suites.

Even longtime M&A practitioners are finding that their expertise and training only partly prepare them to compete fluently in the frothy waters of today's culturally localized markets, and to do it at scale.

On the seller's side of the M&A equation, many business owners are finding they have only an apprentice-level understanding of what it will take to effectively exit their company with the handsome multiples they richly deserve.

Many others feel thrust into sink-or-swim waters of a fast-evolving marketplace and need to swiftly come up to speed on the strategies that best capitalize on emerging realities.

And so, we'll jump right into these strategies—the very strategies that H-E Parts put to work in Chile and at mining sites around the world—the strategies that built a small company into a substantial player on the global stage precisely because of how it aligned with the local cultural realities in each market it served.

1 The Curious Paradox of Global Connectivity

For some four decades now, we've been told by anyone with a pedestal that the business world is *converging* on itself—and with a vengeance. A thousand TV channels. A million internet portals. Wide open markets just hours away by jet transport. Digital platforms for every industry and application. These amazing developments are all purportedly melting away the old cultural boundaries and creating a kind of monocultural marketplace worldwide.

There has been such an obviousness to this notion that to dispute it would seem almost blind, uneducated, undiscerning—pick your poison. But the thing about poisons, I've found, is that everywhere in nature there is an antidote right nearby.

And I'm suggesting that what our world is now truly experiencing is a great paradox. That the more globalized and interconnected the world becomes, the more localized and disconnected it also becomes—with local forces asserting their own autonomy with pride, passion, and plenty of vigor.

As I see it, the world has become like a single prism, if you will. Global forces pass through this prism, and the light splinters into countless vibrant colors embraced by communities in their own unique way. And yes, embraced with vigor. In this sense, the very definition of *local* has taken on an added *primacy*. Understanding and honoring this local primacy is no longer optional; it's mission-critical for most (though certainly not all) companies seeking a global footprint.

Companies running M&A across borders are seeing that deals now succeed or fail not simply on financial modeling or product fit but on how well leaders grasp the *local context* in which the assets live and breathe. That means the winning acquirer in today's environment is often not the one with the deepest pockets but the one with the most nuanced cultural intelligence and ability to apply it. (And by winning, I don't mean simply acquiring a target but making the investment pay out!)

This seeming paradox between increasing globalism and increasing localism hasn't been given the attention I think it truly deserves over the last several decades.

As noted earlier, business analyst Kenichi Ohmae was the first to popularize the notion of an emerging "borderless world" four decades ago. And in his analysis, he found the performance of too many business executives at the time severely lacking …

> *"… too often managers fail to pay attention to the natural boundaries of these cultural units as opposed to industry sector-based units. This is especially true with efforts to diversify out of familiar business lines. Many such efforts miscarry because the people making the decisions are those who grew up in the*

original culture. They ignore the differences in soil that make it possible for different businesses to grow … They want to use common systems, common yardsticks, and common assumptions across their wide range of businesses and across the entire globe. They want to compare things easily using precisely the same yardsticks from product line to product line. They want simplicity. What they get is chaos."

I highly doubt that these managers Ohmae referred to were slothful or lacking in talent. More likely, they were just being human—doing what managers before them had done. Ohmae opened our eyes to this growing managerial problem, and we learned quite a lot from his insights—but we didn't learn enough, apparently.

We certainly didn't learn much from *The New York Times'* bestselling author Thomas Friedman's 2007 book, with its catchy title, *The World Is Flat.* Perhaps he or his publishers were simply seeking a marketing hook to sell books, but the top line was either naive or insight-free. The world was far from metaphorically flat then, farther now.

A better descriptor of our world today could be this: A global superhighway system where every off-ramp drops you into a distinctly local landscape with its own rules, rhythms, and realities.

For those of us in M&A, especially in the lower-middle market, these off-ramps can be seen as barriers or as maps. Maps that don't seek to ignore, paper over, or even adapt to local differences, but instead to navigate local differences artfully—treating each market not as a carbon copy of the last but as a living creature to be understood on its own terms.

Indeed, we're seeing that the future may well belong to enterprises that can scale globally in ambition but locally in practice.

Coming to Grips with the Paradox

Taking the time to truly grasp this seemingly curious paradox has to be Step 1 for any entrepreneur seeking to build a value-creating enterprise that can endure the multicultural complexities of the world's off-ramps.

Whereas mergers and acquisitions have for centuries turned on the familiar levers of capital, technology, and distribution synergies … today, success increasingly depends on something less tangible but far more decisive: the integration of diverse cultural norms, core values, and communication styles across richly varied local markets.

And whereas competitive advantage once stemmed from financial and operational excellence, it must now align the company's global purpose and core values with local cultural needs and sensibilities.

Forward-thinking companies are accomplishing this alignment by building *nested cultures*, locally grounded subcultures, if you will, that extend the company's global ambitions while fully empowering regional identities. This forward-thinking approach allows companies to remain globally coherent yet locally resonant.

So, for instance, in an acquisition, it's no longer enough for the acquirer to audit the balance sheets and run headcounts. Leaders need to devote just as much time to taking a full measure of the newly merged cultures and finding out …

- How will these once different teams now get along and collaborate?
- How will the old lines of authority give way to productive new lines?
- How can two companies' core values become one set of winning values?
- How will this new ecosystem translate into bottom-line results?

In answering these first few of the many cultural intelligence questions, a company will begin developing a plan to thrive in this paradoxical new world—where globalization and localization are in constant tension. But we're getting ahead of ourselves here. Let's step back and quickly review the three leading strategies a CEO and senior management have to choose from when deciding how to compete in today's world.

THE GLOBAL STRATEGY: ONE BRAND, ONE PLAYBOOK

For a number of companies, the Global Strategy remains the gold standard since their competitive edge comes from (a) massive scale, (b) interoperability, and (c) tight-fisted control. These companies operate from a strong corporate center, designing products, managing supply chains, and orchestrating branding from a central office and sending it outward with DO NOT ALTER stickers affixed.

The biggest advantage of this approach is apparent: efficiency. Costs drop, operations streamline, and the customer experience is consistent. A Toyota Corolla is instantly recognizable from Tokyo to Toronto. An iPhone functions the same whether you buy it in Seoul or San Francisco.

Industrial giants such as Caterpillar, GE, Toyota, and ABB exemplify this model, as do tech leaders such as Apple and Microsoft. They leverage a singular global identity, ensuring uniform quality and unified brand promise. For companies with mature brands and global customer bases generating multibillions in revenues, this strategy often delivers the greatest leverage—efficiency and consistency that outweigh any concerns for local nuances. Certainly, local cultural differences still play into marketing and promotion, but only at the margin.

THE MULTIDOMESTIC STRATEGY: LOCAL MARKETS, LOCAL CONTROL

Across the spectrum lies the Multidomestic Strategy, which empowers local subsidiaries to operate as near-independent businesses. Here, decision-making authority resides largely in the individual country or regional offices. Each is allowed to tailor offerings, operations, and marketing to the specific tastes and expectations of local consumers.

This model shines in highly regulated industries where trust, alignment, and compliance are critical to market entry. Industrial giants such as US-based Emerson Electric engineer process automation solutions differently for North America, Europe, and Asia under locally recognized sub-brands and acquired entities. India's Tata Steel operates under the Tata brand globally, but products, pricing, and even supply chains are regionally differentiated. Germany-based Siemens sells turbines, renewables, and transmission that are customized to local power grid codes, energy policies, and the political milieu.

The multidomestic model maximizes local responsiveness but at a cost: duplication of effort. Each market builds its own systems, hires its own teams, and reinvents much of what others are already doing. Efficiency takes a back seat to local cultural fluency.

GLOBAL AIM, LOCAL EXECUTION—CREATING A G.A.L.E. FORCE

Between those two poles lies a more modern synthesis—a Global Aim, Local Execution strategy we sum up as the **G.A.L.E. Force**. This hybrid model seeks to reconcile the benefits of global efficiency with those of local resonance. **G.A.L.E. Force** seeks to standardize that which is strategic, fundamental, and the beneficiary of scale …

while allowing local teams to execute with latitude because they best understood local needs.

Operationally, in the simplest terms, this approach separates back end from front end.

This approach is most readily recognized in companies such as McDonald's. Its supply chain, quality systems, and brand identity are globally standardized. Yet its menu is famously local—the McSpicy Paneer in India, the Ebi Burger in Japan, the McBaguette in France. Starbucks uses a similar approach, maintaining centralized sourcing and training programs but allowing local teams to design store layouts and menu additions that reflect regional culture. L'Oréal goes even further, leveraging global research and production capabilities while aligning marketing and product formulations to local beauty norms.

Among industrial companies, 3M is well known for its global innovation model, yet it distinctly empowers local subsidiaries to develop applications and variants. Similarly, Germany's Bosch provides automotive systems, industrial technology, and tools based on R&D centralized in Renningen but manufactured in sixty-plus countries. And France's Schneider Electric, a leader in energy management and industrial automation ecosystems, deploys a single global architecture with local integrations in one-hundred-plus countries.

My own companies—H-E Parts and Manitex—have operated within this hybrid structure. This has meant building global systems for procurement, innovation, engineering, and operations that ensure discipline and consistency … while deliberately leaving room for local leaders to shape the customer experience and handle local regulatory realities. That flexibility—to understand how a Chilean copper mine operates differently from an Australian coal mine, for instance—has often been a decisive factor in earning the trust and cooperation of our stakeholders.

Choosing the Right Kind of Global Strategy

Breakdown of global expansion strategies				
Strategy Type	Decision Power	Standardization Level	Local Responsiveness	Example Companies
Global	Centralized	High	Low	Caterpillar, GE, Toyota, ABB, Apple, Microsoft
Multidomestic	Fully Decentralized	Low	Hight	Emerson Electric, Tata Steel, Siemens, Nestlé, Unilever, MTV
Global Ambition, Local Execution	Global Systems + Local Autonomy	Medium	Medium-high	3M, Bosch, Schneider Electric, McDonald's, L'Oréal, H-E Parts

A company's senior management and board will usually consider these three strategies and choose the one they believe is best for the company. For those seeking efficiency and control, a Global Strategy is compelling. For industries that demand responsiveness and trust, a Multidomestic Strategy offers essential agility. For firms seeking to scale sustainably across diverse markets, the Global Aim, Local Execution strategy hits the sweet spot—balancing operational discipline with cultural intelligence.

Our focus here will be centered on …

Understanding This G.A.L.E. Force

Business sage Peter Drucker is thought to have chummed the strategy waters in the 1970s with his likely apocryphal but on-theme quip that "Culture eats strategy for breakfast." He did write in *Manage-*

ment: Tasks, Responsibilities, Practices that "culture—no matter how defined—is singularly persistent" and that "management's first task is to make sure that the organization's culture and mission are compatible." Drucker's focus was more on business internal to the marketplace rather than external.

Two decades would pass before sociologist Roland Robertson coined the term *glocalization* in 1992 and took Drucker's thinking into the larger global economy that was then emerging. Robertson argued that global forces could no longer seek to preempt local forces but instead had to *adapt to local* mores and values. His choice of the word *adapt* suggested that big global companies could still run their same old strategies; they just needed to *adapt* a bit. Roberton didn't use the words *conform* or *align*—he used *adapt*.

The shortcomings of this thinking were soon brought to light by Professor Arjun Appadurai in his book *Modernity at Large*. Appadurai thought that the then-emerging uniformity in global culture flows was "disjunctive," that is, lacking connection. So, those cultural flows were most likely to produce some disconnected business experiences in many places around the globe.

And right he was, as that one giant prism we mentioned earlier began splitting local markets into an array of vibrant colors. Companies that ignored or merely sought to adapt to these locally vibrant colors would soon find themselves losing out to other companies who sought to align with them culturally.

That aligning would be the ideal.

The process of aligning a company's local teams with their cultural environs meant that the company could indeed eat strategy—not only for breakfast, but all day long.

This thinking has since gained some purchase in the business community and helped to bolster my own thinking about Global

Aim, Local Execution (the **G.A.L.E. Force**) in the companies I've run and advised.

Ironically, perhaps, this thinking is also being proven out by the ubiquity of social media. For the fact is, companies can now take a message "across the socials" to a global audience with instantaneous speed and targeting precision. But at the same time, local leaders can use social media to elevate and amplify their own region-specific content, languages, and norms. That means a marketing push by a major company could easily be trampled by a lone local influencer who leans on the primacy of local customs and values.

Behavioral economics tells us—has long told us—that trust and loyalty spring full-born from cultural affinity. A brand that feels out of step with the local zeitgeist, even if its quality or price is superior, risks rejection. Far from erasing local identity, globalization has amplified it. And I suspect that people will more and more define themselves by their locality precisely because the world *feels* ever more crowded and homogenized *(even when it's not).*

Acquirers who fail to read these signals can alienate local business owners, as well as their employees and customers, faster than you can say "lost in translation."

Walmart's early attempt to replicate its US retail model in Germany famously collapsed—not because Germans didn't need groceries but because Walmart's enforced cheeriness, bagging policies, and morning pep rallies clashed with local norms.

The logic of localizing at scale is more easily grasped in the retail and fast-food sectors, less so in heavy industrial and technology. Yet the logic equally applies—especially in an M&A context.

Executing Brilliantly with G.A.L.E. Force

Strategy is about execution, essentially, and localized execution allows a company to simultaneously achieve operational breadth and deep cultural resonance. Major efficiencies of scale are still harnessed back at HQ without stepping on the relevance, responsiveness, or rigor required to stand out in each distinct locale.

While globalization emphasizes uniformity for efficiency and consistency, and glocalization stresses adaptation to local conditions, G.A.L.E. takes the best of both. It recognizes that in an interconnected yet culturally diverse marketplace, competitive advantage comes from building commercial architectures that scale intelligently within the boundaries of local customs, mores, idiosyncrasies, everything.

In practice, the **G.A.L.E. Force** may require a reworking of many companies' systems and procedures. Reporting relationships. Decentralized teams. Offer fluidity. Local brand loyalty cultivation. Up and down the value creation chain, there may be changes. All while preserving the efficiencies of the company's central backbone.

When a company enters a new region or country, or merges with a new and distinct culture, it faces a simple truth: What works in one place can fail spectacularly in another. Following the **G.A.L.E. Force** does help by putting forceful local winds at your back, driving the growth in a local organic way. In a many-cultured world, G.A.L.E. is at once a blueprint for local relevance and resilience as well as a method of expansion for fantastic returns.

End of the day, it's all about expanding across regions and markets while embracing local cultures, tastes, and rules. Expanding widely, rooting deeply. Unlike traditional global strategies that impose uniformity, G.A.L.E. aligns with local cultures within a unified global framework—letting each market feel local while benefiting from global resources. In an interconnected world, it's the key to scaling not just efficiently but intelligently and authentically.

SOLVING FOR THE EQUATION: DIVERSITY = IMPACT

When talking about a multicultural world, the subject of *diversity* now follows as uncomfortably as conversations shift to the weather at polite dinner parties.

The concept of diversity—the presence of varied identities, perspectives, and experiences within a workforce—first gained traction in business and political circles in the 1990s. It was long overdue, thoughtful observers can agree. Before long, the very word had become a cultural lightning rod: praised simply for existing, wielded like a political football, seized by those sensing a gravy train leaving the station. It sparked debate, provoked acclaim, and drew scrutiny—all in the normal flow of acculturation. So naturally, business analysts soon began pumping out studies linking diversified workforces to improved corporate performance.

Analysts at Boston Consulting Group found that companies boasting diverse management teams enjoyed 19 percent higher revenues because of their ability to better innovate.

For almost a decade, McKinsey's analysts studied 1,265 companies in twenty-three countries and six global regions. In their latest 2023 study, they found "companies in the top quartile for ethnic and cultural diversity on executive teams are 39 percent more likely to experience above-average profitability." Diversity "fosters innovation, enhances decision-making, and improves financial performance," they said. And more recently, McKinsey added that "leadership diversity is also convincingly associated with holistic growth ambitions, greater social impact, and more satisfied workforces."

Not to be outstatisticized, Vijay Eswaran at the World Economic Forum published an analysis concluding quite simply that "the business case for diversity in the workplace is now overwhelming … in its capacity to foster innovation, creativity and empathy in ways that homogeneous environments seldom do." Eswaran was also keen to insist that diversity "is about more than gender, race and ethnicity. It now includes employees with diverse religious and political beliefs, education, socioeconomic backgrounds, sexual orientation, cultures and even disabilities. Companies are discovering that, by supporting and promoting a diverse and inclusive workplace, they are gaining benefits that go beyond the optics."

What's more, nearly three-quarters of today's workforce is made up of Millennials and Gen Z, and Millennials are flowing into managerial decision-making roles.

While older generations tend to view diversity through the lens of their own upbringing, to Millennials, it just is … and an ideal workplace ought to support diversity. It's called inclusiveness.

These findings and feelings are widely accepted by business leaders, and why not? They strike us as intuitive, sensible, and morally true north on the compass. But as with anything we are asked to swallow whole, it's always useful to taste it first. In that spirit, are these findings on diversity truly (a) accurate and (b) useful?

Let's think about it in terms of American football and team dynamics.

Every professional team has a core mission, and that's to win. To win, it will by definition have a diverse set of strengths. An offensive lineman's core competency is applying strength, lateral quickness, and endurance with the aim of (a) creating a running alley or (b) protecting the quarterback from onrushes. Meanwhile, a wide receiver's core competency is applying speed, agility, and hand-eye coordination to

(a) get open down the field, (b) catch a thrown ball, and (c) gain extra yardage if possible. These skill sets differ a lot, as do other positions on the eleven-man squad. So there's a diverse set of competencies on the team. Do these diverse competencies themselves create a winning team? Or is it the coaches' and players' combined ability to orchestrate these diverse competencies in a unified way?

The answer, obviously, is that diversity by itself doesn't win; unity does.

How about in the circumstances of a marriage? If partners are not united on the basics of child-rearing, for example, how strong will their relationship really be?

With my own situation, I know that my wife has a superpower. She has an intuition with our daughters that I simply do not have. It was on display a few years back, and not in the most delightful way. She was agitated because she thought our then-five-year-old daughter was ill. Most moms have a difficult time relaxing if their child is under duress. My wife was no different; she just knew something was wrong. I thought our daughter was fine. Doctors thought she was fine. There were, after all, no observable symptoms, and two visits to the doctor's office confirmed that she was fine. A week later, we were rushing to the hospital with our daughter suffering full-blown pneumonia. My wife had known it. I hadn't. Doctors missed it too. Her superpower of intuition was diverse from mine. And oh, did we need her set of skills right then.

This pro argument for diversity of skills on the home front is, I believe, readily transferable to the workplace. You want your organization to have a diverse set of skills and viewpoints. You want to celebrate and respect those skills and viewpoints—because different people are going to net you a clearer, broader path forward.

As in sports and marriage, so, too, in business organizations. We need the diversity in skill sets that different people bring. But more importantly, we need a unified strategy to put that diversity to work, executing for impact.

Now let's complicate the equation.

Let's say your company is looking to develop operations in seven countries (as we were at H-E Parts and later Manitex). Isn't a diverse workforce going to be something of a given? After all, if a US company decides to use local talent to populate their operations in Chile, as we did, isn't that putting diversity first?

Well, actually, it's about something greater than diversity, greater than unity even; it is about culture.

In business, an effective nested culture rarely emerges by luck or happenstance. It is built piece by piece, like a human Lego assembly. It involves deliberate steps, consistent behaviors, and a shared set of beliefs. It results in a more cohesive operation marked by greater collaboration, greater innovation, greater resilience, and greater profitability.

So the success of the organization lies not necessarily in the diversity of its talent, but most necessarily in how its members work together in a shared culture, unified by mutual trust, constant communication, and a guiding purpose. This is what earns the team recognition among their industry peers as a high-performing team.

This is, in my view, indisputable. While academics and business leaders can debate the terms and conditions of modern commerce, who can deny the value of an organization being culturally aligned with its shareholders—whether involved in M&A activity or not?

GETTING TO THE RIGHT EQUATION: UNITY = IMPACT

A diversified-unified culture acts as the connective tissue between strategic intentions and go-to-market behavior. It becomes a strategic multiplier. To make the multiplication happen in an M&A context, forward-thinking leaders will take key actions …

- Architect a diversified-unified culture even before approaching the integration phase of a deal, and then build local DNA into postmerger planning rather than defaulting to the old uniformity.
- Extend and interpret the company's core values into the local vernacular—auguring greater employee engagement and customer satisfaction.
- Aim to turn each local office or facility into a self-sufficient nested culture within the company's global network.
- Become an expert in anticipating potential cultural flashpoints even before they arise, and proactively managing them—lest they fester into lost opportunities.
- Build a culturally intelligent company that navigates differences in communication, etiquette, and style—so that relationships are stronger across the organization.
- Allow local nested cultures to feel safe enough, so they push innovation upward, from local to global, keeping the organization flexible to local needs and desires.

We'll dig into each of these actions later in the book, beginning in chapter 2 with a recounting of how H-E Parts put the **G.A.L.E. Force** to work, literally from the ground up.

M&A Strategy in a Multicultural Age

Before a Tesla or iPhone is manufactured or a skyscraper rises to the sky, the story begins far below our feet. Across the sun-blasted Australian Outback, the copper-rich Andes in South America, or the cold tundra of Northern Alberta, Canada, mining companies are carving the raw ingredients of modern life out of ancient mineral belts.

These companies generate $1.2 trillion in commerce annually, and they are remarkable in their concentration.

A small constellation of multinational firms holds most of the world's mineral rights and channels lithium, copper, iron ore, gold, and other minerals and raw earths into the global commodity markets. Each shipment and traded contract feeds a worldwide marketplace where the earth's most fundamental resources become the currency of progress.

However concentrated, it's an industry of striking contrasts.

Gold miners such as Barrick and Newmont may process up to 250 tons of rock just to extract a single ounce of gold (which is like churning through an apartment building of dirt to get a golf ball-sized chunk of gold). These operations are in some of the most remote locations on the planet. They are self-sufficient and necessitate a decentralized structure with each mine acting as a self-contained unit, shipping out a small but valuable product each day. Often, the product goes out in a pickup truck!

Coal or iron miners such as Peabody Energy or Vale deliver product in bulk. Their product is typically delivered to port, by train or boat, and holds another extreme. These businesses have complex, centralized logistics machines sending trainloads of product each day to port terminals where bulk carriers—some too large to fit through the Panama Canal—wait to transport that product to the world's power plants and steel mills.

Whether mining high-value ounces or low-value tons, the common denominator is the relentless motion of machinery. Each mine site is responsible for efficiently extracting minerals from the rock and dirt, and the mines never sleep. Haul trucks, shovels, and crushers run twenty-four hours a day, seven days a week. Any downtime can ripple through the entire supply chain, idling multimillion-dollar assets and thousands of workers. Capacity utilization and production reliability are not just metrics; they are survival factors in the mining business.

This machinery ecosystem creates stability as well as frustration for mine operators. With scant competition, the original equipment manufacturers (OEMs) can seem like monopolies. Miners depend on these machines and a close relationship with the OEMs, but the relationship can strain when service or pricing feels one-sided. It's what miners half-jokingly call their "love–hate marriage with Caterpillar." They may want to leave the relationship, but they cannot.

Where H-E Parts Found an Opening

This is the love–hate world that H-E Parts stepped into. The miners' total dependence on expensive machinery, along with the industry's high barriers to entry, limited numbers of customers, and narrow operating margins, meant one thing in our view:

Even small gains in reliability or cost could have an impact.

Every mine site is measured on productivity and very slim margins. Therefore, efficiency, equipment uptime, and reliability were critical factors at every location. If we could deliver even small gains to the equipment performance, the mine operators ought to welcome us. If we could innovate solutions that would prolong component life and increase uptime ratios, total cost of ownership would decline, as would risk. Perhaps most importantly, we wouldn't be competing head-to-head with the OEMs, but rather enhancing and even complementing them. We'd be the BASF of mining—not manufacturing the equipment, but making the equipment better.

A billboard at the Fort McMurray International Airport sharing H-E Parts' core vision

This idea of ours was simple but disruptive.

Instead of trying to sell through traditional dealer networks, we'd go directly to the mines. Our engineers and technicians would get into the dirt right alongside mine managers to diagnose the problems they faced, and to tailor real fixes. If a mine in the Alberta oil sands was struggling with seal failures at –40°F, we'd redesign the seals for cold-weather resilience. If bearings wore out prematurely, we'd engineer preload settings that extended their life by thousands of hours. Unlike the OEMs who had to manage an average of 35,000 stock keeping units (SKUs), we'd focus on the handful of SKUs that truly mattered, the mission-critical components that kept billion-dollar operations churning 24/7.

When we launched down this path, the global market for surface-mining parts and remanufacturing services was estimated at about

$3.7 billion, or 0.31 percent of the whole mining industry—so ideal for a niche operator, we believed.

Yet at the time, the big OEMs controlled the vast majority of the equipment parts and maintenance market. Our challenge was to carve out a little slice of this big mining pie by delivering a unique combination of reliability, speed, trust, and most importantly, innovation.

Developing an Innovation-Centric Strategy

When I joined H-E Parts, the company had less than 2 percent share of the global equipment mining parts market. It was a good business, but far from a great business.

We set out to build a great business that would grow to over $30 million in EBITDA. Applying a reasonable eight-times EBITDA exit multiple would impute an enterprise value of roughly $240 million. At that valuation, equity investors could see a handsome return on their original investment—a compelling story.

We began with a crisp statement of what we wanted H-E Parts to become—that is, what our mission would be going forward. We distilled these objectives down into their purest form …

1. Provide solutions that maximize uptime for mission-critical surface-mining equipment at a minimum lifetime cost to the mine operators.
2. Become the leading independent provider of aftermarket parts, components, and remanufacturing services to the surface-mining industry.

To accomplish this 1–2 waterfall, we would have to distinguish ourselves in a large and fragmented market that looked upon little guys like us as unreliable. We had to remove risk and create value that would differentiate us from the OEMs. Although mines are owned by global companies, the mines themselves are decentralized. So we would have to invest in both our ability to innovate product solutions and a delivery mechanism that could scale and impress these decentralized mine operators.

More specifically, that would mean H-E Parts would have to …

- Innovate solutions and high-quality (differentiated) products.
- Be local enough to effectively engage the individual mine sites.
- Grow to meet customer expectations of capability.
- Secure our supply chain.
- Unify the brand and H-E Parts story.

In so doing, we believed, we could be viewed by potential customers as an attractive alternative to the existing OEM solutions.

An option for doing this was the grassroots approach, entering each market organically and opening an H-E Parts store to serve a cluster of mines. However, this would take too long. Instead, we chose to acquire small, independent companies that would complement our goal while giving us a regional platform for growth.

We looked at each of these required capabilities that we needed to master and organized them into four strategic priorities to be pursued with 110 percent of our focus.

- **Complementary acquisitions.** Consider acquisitions that enhance H-E Parts' position in a mission-critical product category (within debt-load constraints).
- **Intense customer focus.** Leverage existing customer relationships to gain increased credibility as a trustworthy alternative to the OEMs.

- **Platform validation.** Demonstrate that H-E Parts is an integrated company with both attractive growth margins and resistance to market downturns.
- **Localized products.** Demonstrate the ability to transfer products/technologies across a global platform to the satisfaction of locally focused customers.

Delivering on these priorities would require us to pursue a strategy that was relatively foreign to the mining industry. No easy undertaking.

PURSUING A STRATEGY NEW TO THE INDUSTRY

As noted, H-E Parts was founded by JP Richard, a man dedicated to an M&A buildup he hoped would bring together operating units in seven countries to become the largest independent provider of aftermarket parts, components, and remanufacturing services—principally in the mining industry.

Left to right: Steve McBrayer, Michael Coffey, and JP Richard celebrating an acquisition closing at our corporate headquarters

In short order, H-E Parts would indeed acquire fourteen companies to achieve JP's vision. But in the early days, it was far from clear sailing.

Breaking into the mining industry, which is highly consolidated with a few operators doing almost everything, is tough. Anyone seeking to do more than sell sandwiches to the miners would have to develop some kind of direct-to-mine strategy that got them through the very locked mining gates. Mine sites are not accessible to the public, for obvious reasons. Every visitor and vendor requires an invitation.

We would have to get an invitation, for starters. And then we'd have to overcome quality-control concerns, existing dependencies on the OEMs, difficult maintenance agreements or procurement contracts, and the perceived risk of doing business with a newcomer. Most products require a complex test to evaluate and validate product reliability. Quite a challenge!

For perspective, just one hour of lost time at a gold mine costs the mine operator more than $100,000.

Time is very literally money. A mine operator is not going to budge off the status quo unless the status quo is not working.

So, going directly to mine operators with our little solutions could be a dicey proposition. "Innovators are the ones with the arrows in their backs" is how the expression goes, and not without merit. In mining, nobody had made a serious business solely out of aftermarket parts and remanufacturing, much less trying to sell that proposition directly. There was bound to be some pain.

But JP had a vision, or at least he had an itch. He had previously been at the helm of Massey Ferguson and AGCO, manufacturers of farm tractors that could last for fifty or sixty years. They'd sell those tractors for a small profit and make their real money replacing worn-out parts. It was a savvy business model.

But then entrepreneurs figured it out. They came in and tried to steal the parts business by undercutting, reducing cost or quality, whatever it took. JP was perennially frustrated with these "pirates," but couldn't beat them with his incumbent business model. So he decided to become a pirate himself, and thus, H-E Parts.

By the time I joined H-E Parts in 2008, first as a COO and later as CEO, the company was off on an acquisition spree. Our plan at the time called for growth and expansion, acquiring three major companies in 2008, just before the global financial crisis. These acquisitions gave us a foothold in Australia and introduced key product lines in mobile equipment maintenance as well as crusher maintenance. The plan was ambitious, and we would ultimately shoot well beyond those optimistic forecasts. We would attribute a good measure of that success to our acquisition of a little mining services operation in the Chilean Andes.

ACQUIRING MORGAN TOOK US DEEP INTO THE ANDES

Morgan manufactured clutches and brakes for heavy equipment. It had been around since 1943, and was then acquired by Roger Robillard, who took the business from Canada to Chile and then Peru. We looked at Robillard's company first in 2008, and didn't invest, but only because of the global financial meltdown and corporate financials that weren't quite strong enough. Only later, in 2013, did we acquire Morgan. And though it didn't have a complementary product line or service capabilities, it was in the right place with the right customer base (the key to going direct).

Morgan's Chilean operations were opened and run by Alfonso Teplizky, and set up as an authorized distributor for global product lines. It later added onsite hydraulic services and even operated a mining truck-sized wash bay for the largest mine site in Chile, BHP's Escondida. Morgan did not have the highly engineered mission-critical parts we had, but acquiring Morgan gave us a foothold. It was already inside the gates and had service contracts at eight Chilean mining operations. Moreover, Alfonso had built a great management team that was operating profitably. Three big synergies.

In evaluating potential acquisitions such as Morgan, H-E Parts had developed a table of necessary criteria. In particular, there were five criteria we were seeking to fill. We called these the legs of the table, and we sought to have at least three of them present to move forward with an acquisition.

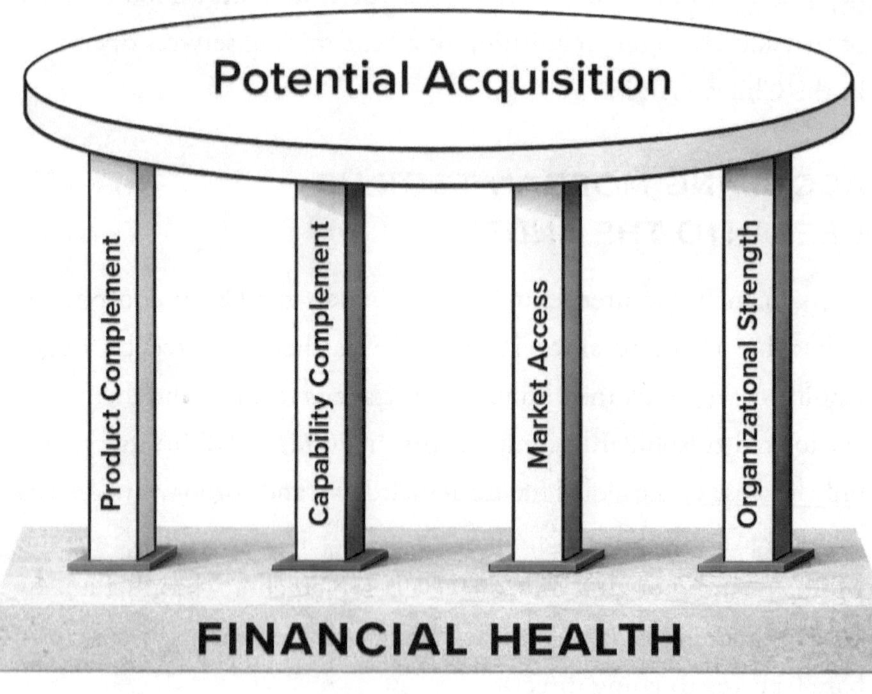

Evaluating a Potential Acquisition

1. Product Complement

The acquired product line naturally extends or strengthens our company's existing portfolio, fits with our existing relationships of value, expands our presence in adjacent or high-growth categories, or unlocks new solutions for our customers.

2. Capability Complement

When the acquisition is added to the platform, it broadens what we can do operationally with our remanufacturing expertise, engineering talent, supply chain channels, and global distribution network. We net a more scalable, more competitive, more resilient platform.

3. Market Access

Achieving meaningful scale is always about reinvention, so the acquisition should newly enable the company to enter new markets, penetrate deeper in priority geographies, or mature the company's systems and processes. Scale isn't just about gaining size. It's about gaining new leverage, efficiency, or credibility in critical markets.

4. Organizational Strength

Since we'll want to grow the company quickly, it must have the right talent and depth of bench that facilitates this.

5. Financial Health

As a start-up operation ourselves, we can't turn around a business that's not profitable. Therefore, we look for targets that are healthy and profitable, with a strong balance sheet, stable cash flow, and predictable earnings that provide a solid foundation for integration without undue risk or untenable liabilities.

So, these were the summary criteria we used at H-E Parts to decide whether a business was a fit for us. Acquiring Morgan gave us only three of the five legs. But that was enough since it got us through the mine gates right away, rather than the years it might have taken otherwise. It was rather essential to our direct strategy, actually.

This acquisition of Morgan led to the Codelco–Komatsu story we looked at earlier. Recall that Chile's state-owned mining giant, Codelco, was expanding in southern Chile, and its oldest mine site was moving into a new phase of underground mining. Its surface fleet could be retired or refurbished, and Codelco was looking for an economical way to expand at its Salvador division. Codelco believed its fleet of Komatsu ultraclass haul trucks had more life to give. It needed to prepare the trucks to work reliably at Salvador and was facing a massive $50 million refurbishing contract, with Komatsu as the favored vendor.

But that contract went to H-E Parts because we had acquired Morgan's team, which understood the local mining culture and had already earned the trust and respect needed to "credentialize" our innovative solutions. The efforts of our local teams most certainly validated the value of our "global aim, local execution" strategy that we'll talk more about.

COMMITTING TO BEING THE INNOVATOR IS A CONSTANT CHALLENGE

A year after the Morgan acquisition, our Chilean regional manager, Alfonso, proposed that we bid on a large truck maintenance contract at Codelco Chile. The contract was multiyear and large, and it would give us daily access within the mine. Important things. But the contract focused on cab maintenance and cleaning. Essentially, it was a labor contract to assist the mine with seat belt changes and cleaning the truck cabs. This work, although important to the mine, did not align with our strategy. The parts were not mission-critical, offered no opportunities for innovation or differentiation, and would not allow us to remanufacture or find performance-improvement opportunities.

After reviewing the agreement, I asked Alfonso how this janitorial contract matched our global strategy and core values. He admitted that the contract did not fit, but he remained attracted to the multimillion-dollar opportunity.

Our company tagline was firmly locked in by then. It was *Innovation, Not Duplication.* We didn't design things; we made them work better. That was our sweet spot.

Alfonso's heart was in the right place. His focus was on the customer. But he wanted to bid on a contract that didn't fit our core value of innovation. Our products solved very real problems in very unique ways. But this was janitorial services. We weren't going to add any value. During a teleconference with Alfonso and his Chilean team, it was easy to see that our conversations were not going to sway the team's determination to bid on this work. They were relentless in their efforts to convince me that this was a good pursuit. I admired their ambition, but the project was simply outside our core competency.

I asked Alfonso to meet again in one week. And beforehand, I wanted him to review the opportunity not from a profitability standpoint, but to outline how this contract would meet our strategy and help us to grow our reputation as a market leader in innovation.

A week later, he couldn't, and we didn't bid. The contract would have consumed valuable capital and resources, hindering our ability to pursue more favorable work. Sometimes the best deal you do is the one you don't do.

On my next visit to Chile, we reviewed this bid again and used it as an opportunity to reinforce our strategy and core values. The purpose was to fortify the importance of our company's culture and core values for the Chilean team. To help them see how we were building a nested culture, a culture in which a diverse group of people unified by core values could perform at their very best.

On that visit, we all came together in Antofagasta to cook dinner together—an event that would continue on each of my visits. In that meeting, I didn't have to tell the team "No" (which can be problematic in Latin cultures). I had to let them see how that contract didn't really fit with our company culture of innovation, so, ultimately, it wasn't going to advance our interests. In fact, it might distract us and even become a net negative for us.

The value of these team culture meetings didn't become clear until two years later, when Alfonso landed the biggest contract we'd ever received, from that same customer. It was a significant contract and ultimately profitable because it hit our sweet spot. Alfonso turned his understanding of the customer's needs, along with his now-clearer understanding of our company's culture of innovation, into a big win for us.

Remaining true to a strategy, like remaining true to your school, tends to work just fine until temptations arise. Every business faces temptations, and the tastiest of them is usually the prospect of a quick buck. Who wants to turn away money? That's why we decided to put a hard and fast policy in place at H-E Parts:

Once a year, we would assess our entire operation to ensure that the long-term strategy was still working. If it was, then the topic would be taken off the table for another year. No exceptions. This assessment became our annual strategy and planning meeting. Its participants were the executive committee, essentially, my direct reports from around the world. These meetings at H-E Parts and later with

Manitex were both powerful and influential for the business and for me personally.

Here's another example of how this kind of rigid adherence to our strategy and core values paid off for H-E Parts.

MAKING A STRATEGY OF INNOVATION PAY OFF MULTICULTURALLY

The Birrana acquisition included strengthening the engineering culture.
Left to right: Paul Ingleton, Ashley Hams, Michael Coffey, Peter French, Rhys Bowkett, Lee Houghton, and Simon David

Another one of our 2008 acquisitions was the Australian company Birrana, which gave us another foothold and some cool symbology as well. "Birrana" is the Aboriginal term for a "throwing stick" that has some boomerang-type qualities useful in hunting. It fit with Birrana's engineering philosophy of giving heavy equipment wheel-end and suspension systems a second life when otherwise that equipment may have been written off. What others saw as worn-out parts, Birrana saw as opportunities to engineer better performance a second time around.

So, with Birrana and H-E Parts joined, the message became one of innovation that delivered reliability back to our customers, sustainability back to the industry, and lasting value back to the machines that move great volumes. We soon had the chance to prove out this messaging with no less a company than Caterpillar.

Long the leader in heavy equipment, Caterpillar's big haul trucks run on a mechanical drive that's dependable in most conditions, but typical component life is only thirteen thousand hours. Since they run pretty much 24/7, that's only about two years of uptime. And since they cost about $4 million apiece, mine operators are keen to ratchet every hour they can out of them.

So in continuing with H-E Parts' direct-to-mine strategy, we dispatched our newly acquired Birrana engineers from the coal basins of Northern Queensland to the coal basins of Wyoming. On site at Peabody Energy's largest operation, North Antelope Rochelle Mine (NARM), was a huge fleet of Caterpillar trucks. We had an idea for those trucks, and though we were still a small vendor, we knew it was a big idea the operator would want to hear.

We proposed that instead of taking the big Cats out of rotation for costly and frequent wheel end overhauls as planned, we could evaluate a series of enhancements that could extend the life. The Birrana engineers had worked for decades to develop forty-two enhancements, some process-based and some that could be added a la carte to the components. The applications of these Birrana enhancements were designed to extend life and lower costs. We later found that these enhancements improved component hours to thirty-two thousand at this site.

A look at H-E Parts enhancements inside a Caterpillar drive

We offered to test one truck and prove out our value proposition. Peabody Energy's engineers were intrigued by the depth of product knowledge and professionalism that the Australian team brought. And so they offered us an opportunity to try three sets of H-E Parts–Birrana–enhanced wheel groups. We would monitor them jointly and assess their performance. A tenured Peabody Energy engineer was assigned to work with us, and we thought this would launch us into a very quick expansion.

Unfortunately, our US business on point for this project did not follow the Birrana repair plan to the letter. The unit, Crown Parts and Machinery out of Billings, Montana, had also been acquired in 2008. It was a year of significant expansion. We acquired CME (Crushing and Mining Equipment), Birrana Engineering, and Crown Parts and Machinery. The marriage looked promising. Birrana was heavily invested in Caterpillar remanufactured components. Crown

Parts was heavily invested in Komatsu truck replacement parts and hydraulic cylinder repair. However, the DNA of the businesses differed in significant ways. Birrana was born of engineers who would focus on remanufacturing processes and improvements. Crown Parts was founded as a parts company with a distribution model.

The Australia-based and Montana-based businesses had great respect for each other, but naturally, they each defaulted to their roots. Crown Parts did not see the value of Birrana's minute and even pedantic repair protocols. For example, Birrana called for every brake spring to be tested in the repair. There were differences in distributed parts agreements as well. Birrana was using a proprietary friction material, developed jointly with a European manufacturer. Crown Parts was a distributor for a US-based manufacturer of brake supplies.

The Birrana components performed well, but we were unable to maximize the engagement with Peabody Energy for several years to come. The cultural differences between our business units created hurdles that were difficult to navigate and slow to overcome.

THE RELENTLESS ART OF HORIZONTAL EXPANSION

Our founder, JP, had a single-minded drive to acquire every company in our space that could extend our global footprint. JP's enthusiasm was a big positive, but not without its negatives. For example, the industry's biggest trade show, the MINExpo, was coming up, and we were super excited to attend. These industry get-togethers only happen every four years because it can take five months to assemble and then disassemble these big machines, transport them to the convention center, reassemble for showing, and then take them back down and ship them home. It costs millions of dollars for the big companies just to show off their wares.

MINExpo, like other tradeshows, is an opportunity to meet everyone in the industry at one location. Relationships are rekindled or forged at these events, and we were looking to discover and engage potential acquisition targets. Our senior leadership team—JP Richard, Steve McBrayer (CFO and later CEO), Ian Olivieri (Managing Director Australia), and I—were to lead internal meetings with our team. And we had a list of potential targets to introduce ourselves to. JP and Ian went to pay a visit to the booth of an engine repair company. To Ian, it was an opportunity to make an introduction and fact find. JP was far more direct; he approached an engineer and asked to see the owner since he was interested in buying the company.

Upon returning to our H-E Parts booth, Ian was downcast. "You can't just go around offering to buy people's companies," Ian addressed us all. "It's simply too direct, and we'll turn them off or insult them, harming our chances of making a deal."

Steve, Ian, and I were in agreement on that.

Left to right: Ian Olivieri, Michelle Robless, and Steve McBrayer

Soon enough, JP returned with something of a smirk on his face. He glanced over our shoulders, and we turned to see the engine rebuilding company owners approaching our booth—eager to speak with us. When they left later, JP turned to us with words to the effect of, "Kids, this is how it's done." JP believed the business would be a good fit, so he offered to buy it. Very direct.

Or was it too direct?

Probably both. Because an offer to buy without a good round of strategic due diligence is a powder keg situation. One that usually begins with the acquirer saying, "Don't worry, nothing's going to change," and the acquiree saying, "Good, because I built a great company and I don't want it to change; it's my legacy, after all." But now it was up to the lieutenants—which included me, in this case—to figure out what would happen next. Most often, when one company acquires another, there are going to be changes.

You want there to be changes—both small and large.

One of the worst things you can do is buy a company and leave it alone. There are plenty of reasons for this, as we'll see, but the main reason is that in a merger or acquisition, you have two different cultures becoming one.

Most people think of culture as geographically dependent, based on the usual suspects—language, shared heritage, music, art, and similar geographic factors. Culture, however, is developed when a group of people spends enough time together. It coalesces where habits and common practices become the unspoken rule. Countries have distinct cultures. Cities have distinct cultures. I can tell you that the culture of Billings is very different from that of New York City. Companies, too, have differing cultures. They are based on a founder's vision, values, and historical circumstances. The merging of two companies is also a merger of two cultures. This is magnified when acquiring businesses located in different countries. In the case of H-E Parts, we were merging the cultures of seven countries and fourteen operating entities.

The languages people use, and their ethnic backgrounds, are evident pieces of a multicultural mosaic, yes. But they are not nearly as important in a business context as is the nested culture that a company can create for itself.

This becomes especially evident when one company culture is joined with another, and you have a multicultural experience at the beginning. In managing this joining, there cannot help but be changes if the two cultures are to combine their diversified talent sets and unify into a new and productive nested culture.

Operationally, this is about creating a culture within a culture.

This nested culture does not seek to replace, but to complement. And it can unite the newly merged companies in profound ways.

BRINGING TWO VERY DIFFERENT BUSINESSES TOGETHER

The acquisition of Birrana and Crown Parts became a perfect fit for the H-E Parts strategy, but it took time. The Australian outfit's technical DNA ran deep in large-scale machining and manufacturing for mining equipment drive train systems. All their engineers fancied protractors and compasses in their pocket protectors. We joked at the precision with which one engineer would spread Vegemite on his morning toast. These Australians weren't satisfied unless they could look a problem in the eye and figure out an elegant solution to it.

It was a perfect fit for the H-E Parts strategy that would come to pass. But at the time, that strategy was still a work in progress. Our burden became one of combining Birrana's brilliant engineers with the Billings-based Crown Parts distributors we'd recently acquired. The two crews had little in common other than working in the mining industry. In any given situation, the Adelaide crew would default to designing a better mousetrap, while the Billings crew just wanted to catch a lot of mice. Completely different cultures.

From the outset, we wrestled with the two problems cobbled-together companies face …

- How could two business cultures that were almost exactly halfway around the world from each other, with different regulatory mindsets and different operating structures, be expected to address shared problems in the marketplace?
- How were we going to get these two businesses to collaborate, coordinate, and behave as a unified culture in order to justify our cost of acquisition?

We did it the only way we could at the time, frankly.

We looked at both businesses and tallied up the strengths of each. The more those relative strengths complemented H-E Parts' strategic direction that we'd begun figuring out, the more we valued those strengths. So basically, we assigned values to strengths. The high-valued strengths got our attention; the low-valued strengths did not. And we made sure those high-value strengths were highlighted in every communication with both teams—constant reminders to keep on focus.

It wasn't always easy. But in time, we did get clear on our strategic vision for H-E Parts. The diversified, unified culture that we sought did become the daily marching orders for us all. In time, *Innovation, Not Duplication* became a phrase that epitomized who we were. That mantra would guide all of our decisions. In the consistency of this value creation, the strategy would be executed.

SETTING UP ACQUIRED BUSINESSES TO CREATE VALUE

Caterpillar is a well-known brand to most people. Its Japanese competitor, Komatsu, is less well-known outside of the industry, but both are standout makers of big haul trucks. The two have battled for market share throughout the world as either number one or two in every market. Over the years, Caterpillar designed and perfected a mechanical drive truck. Komatsu, however, opted for a diesel-electric drive train. Similar to a locomotive engine, Komatsu's systems were complex yet efficient. Caterpillar insourced its components and systems, while Komatsu used outside vendors, such as Cummins for its diesel engines and General Electric for its traction motors. Both manufacturers had similar wet disc braking systems and hydraulic systems for steering and for hoisting the dump bed from the truck.

Komatsu 930E Front Corner Assembly Cut-Away used at MINExpo Tradeshow

I'm sharing this background on Caterpillar and Komatsu because it would come into play in the years after we integrated Birrana and Crown Parts, and began to bring their two very different cultures together. It happened when I was visiting customers in Chile. It turned out that two different customers in a single week were experiencing challenges with their Komatsu 930E's steering axle bearing life. Failures were occurring on both new and rebuilt components, and at very low operating hours. I took notes and recall ringing our US-based engineering manager, Ken Pitman. I relayed what I had heard to Ken, expecting that the problem was a fluke within Chile or potentially the result of haul road conditions.

Ken had just recently returned to our Billings office after a visit with Cloud Peak Energy (since sold to NTEC). While at their mining site, Ken had noticed that the Komatsu 930E haul trucks there were having similar bearing failures. He began detailing to me all that he knew about these failures. At the time, we were unclear on the root cause but wanted to learn more. The next week, we set about calling customers with fleets of Komatsu 930E haul trucks and found that the "failing front corner bearings issue" was widespread.

In this kind of situation, the H-E Parts strategy could shine.

If our response to this very critical problem with the Komatsus had been to duplicate our way toward a solution instead of innovating one, we would have (a) copied the specs of the OEM design, (b) tried to replicate the problem in order to figure out the flaw, and (c) tried to fix it. The same approach that every other parts company would try.

There could be worse approaches. Komatsu was and is, after all, a world-class truck manufacturer—even though there was a flaw in their design. Working with them to find a solution was an option. But instead, we devised a plan.

We rallied all the engineers we could and put them on planes to nine mining sites around the world to inspect the trucks on the ground. Shortly thereafter, we had the firsthand data we needed and could confirm that the exact same flaw revealed itself in –40°F Edmonton and 100°F Arizona as well, at thirteen thousand feet in Peru, and again at sea level in Australia. Same problem, every market, every truck.

Unlike our original rollout of the Birrana technology in the US, this time, our Australian and US engineering teams went to work in unison. Progress was accelerated by the now head of North American operations, Bill Brown. I recruited Bill to lead what was Crown Parts, to improve scale, and to bring stronger levels of cooperation to other North American acquired businesses. Bill was an exceptional collaborator, an invaluable skill set for this project's success. Komatsu's original design used common hydraulic oil to both cool the brakes and lubricate the wheel bearings. Our engineers figured out that the oil being used in the trucks' wheel bearings should run at 110°F–120°F, but the oil used in the brake housings could run as high as 180°F. A wide variance, right? Yet there was no variance in oil temperatures on those Komatsu trucks. The shared oil was lightweight and insufficient to adequately lubricate bearings that would support and steer a three-hundred-ton haul truck. The viscosities and temperatures weren't right, which wreaked havoc on the bearings, and the wheels were falling apart in as little as six months.

Now that we knew the problem, we could devise a solution. We turned to a technology we had previously developed for Caterpillar that had proven itself in a similar application, and we modified it for Komatsu. Cloud Peak had a mobile equipment reliability team led by Kelly Gangestad. Prior to joining Cloud Peak, Kelly built a reputation as a foremost expert on electric motors and traction drive systems. His team was charged with finding opportunities to lower costs through improved performance and reliability. Kelly had a long-standing relationship with Ken, strong enough to allow us to run a beta test. The first test would be back at Cloud Peak, where this all began.

Over several weeks, in the heat of the summer, we measured brake performance and operating temperatures of the new system. Our design separated the cooling oil from the bearing oil, and we included Birrana-developed enhancements previously proven out on Caterpillar applications. The difference was significant. We began a program to convert Cloud Peak's Komatsus, and the product quickly became one of H-E Parts' biggest success stories. The design, tested in Wyoming, received a patent in 2015 and can be found on Komatsu 930E trucks from Australia to Chile and Peru. In my view, this success validated our strategy and what we were trying to accomplish at H-E Parts.

Perfecting the M&A Buildup

Even before our senior team at H-E Parts got clear on our strategic focus, we were committed to an M&A buildup to become an industry leader with a platform for acquiring the best players in our space. In private equity, this buildup is also known as *platforming* because the company's first acquisition serves as a platform or foundation upon which smaller, complementary businesses can be added.

The goal of a buildup or platforming is straightforward: Consolidate a fragmented industry, increase scale through calculated reinvention, then capture a premium when the larger entity is eventually sold.

A platform company with meaningful revenue, a strong management team, proven processes, and scalable systems is going to fetch a much higher multiple when sold.

Building the platform itself tends to be more expensive at first, but then subsequent acquisitions can usually come at a lower cost and can be integrated more efficiently, generating operational synergies that ratchet up value creation. With H-E Parts, having a platform made it increasingly easier to convince acquisition targets to join us. And as our success grew, with each new closing, the integration process also grew smoother and easier.

Despite the many financial advantages of a buildup, it also carries risks. The biggest risk is that a buildup can be more difficult to manage than straight "bolt-on" acquisitions. But by focusing on three risk areas, the buildup can be turned into a virtual money machine. Those three risks are …

1. **Acquisition target sourcing.** Identifying targets that can seamlessly join the platform is critical. Poor sourcing drains time, energy, and capital, which can undermine the overall returns.
2. **Market disruptions.** Economic, regulatory, or competitive shifts can lower valuation multiples and extend investment timelines, while also reducing returns. These externalities are by definition outside the company's control; they're wild cards that still have to be played. At H-E Parts, we could not anticipate the global financial crisis of 2008 or the oil recession of 2014–15 setting our plans back.
3. **Postmerger integration.** Merging a company onto the platform means harmonizing back-office functions to drive efficiencies, consolidating front-office operations to eliminate duplications, rebranding to capture expanded market presence capabilities, and most importantly, aligning cultures to boost morale and performance. It's a lot of work!

But with these risks effectively managed, over time, the platform can mature into the endgame of value creation: multiple arbitrage.

Smaller companies usually trade at lower multiples than larger ones, and so consolidating smaller companies onto a single larger platform drives up the valuation multiple. It turns what were modest individual businesses into a far more valuable whole. This is how successful buildups unlock the big eye-popping eight- to ten-times multiples that private equity and ambitious operators seek. This is multiple arbitrage at work.

At H-E Parts, we had perfect sponsors for our buildup. Frontenac of Chicago and Champ Ventures of Sydney were the leads. They adeptly challenged us to refine our strategy (the one we've been talking about here). Steve McBrayer, our first CFO who later succeeded JP Richard as CEO in 2014, drove the effort to define a strategy map for the company.

This strategy setting began, as I've said, with getting clear on our vision and core values.

This clarity was crucial. We needed to put our vision and core values on paper—clearly and visually—so that everyone in the organization could recognize them and follow them. Drawing on the principles of Robert Kaplan and David Norton's Balanced Scorecard, we created a Strategy Map that articulated our strategy in a way that could be broadly understood.

Steve was relentless in his insistence on this discipline, driven by a simple belief: If every employee did not understand the strategy, it would never truly take hold. Regardless of the merits of our strategy, we knew that without clear communication and adoption across the organization, our progress would be slow.

One of the most insightful reviews I ever received was from Doug Black, CEO of Old Castle Materials. Doug, a West Pointer and former Army officer, was highly disciplined. Old Castle Materials acquired the company I was working for, and I found myself promoted to Vice

President, Equipment Services. This was a new position, and although I did not work closely with Doug, I reported directly to him. His review sparkled because of timely insight and the challenge he put to me: Develop a strategic plan for the Equipment Division, at the time a $1.1 billion cost center. His challenge was to the point, weighty, and surprisingly relevant.

The result of Doug's challenge to me came to be known as "10 & 10 by 2010," a strategic plan to improve fleet utilization by 10 percent and reduce fleet operating costs by 10 percent within four years. Our team put in place monthly measures to monitor our progress against these objectives, and it really mattered because the 10 percent cost reduction alone could be worth more than $100 million to the company.

In every business since, I have sought to develop and communicate a clear strategic plan (road map). I've tried to create this clear visual of the company's strategic vision and later couple it with core values—vital to harnessing a common language and set of principles that govern disparate operating units.

As I said, we called the H-E Parts plan our Strategy Map, and I used every opportunity I had with the team to walk them through the map. The following is a single slide from the presentation on the map that I would give to H-E Parts teams around the world.

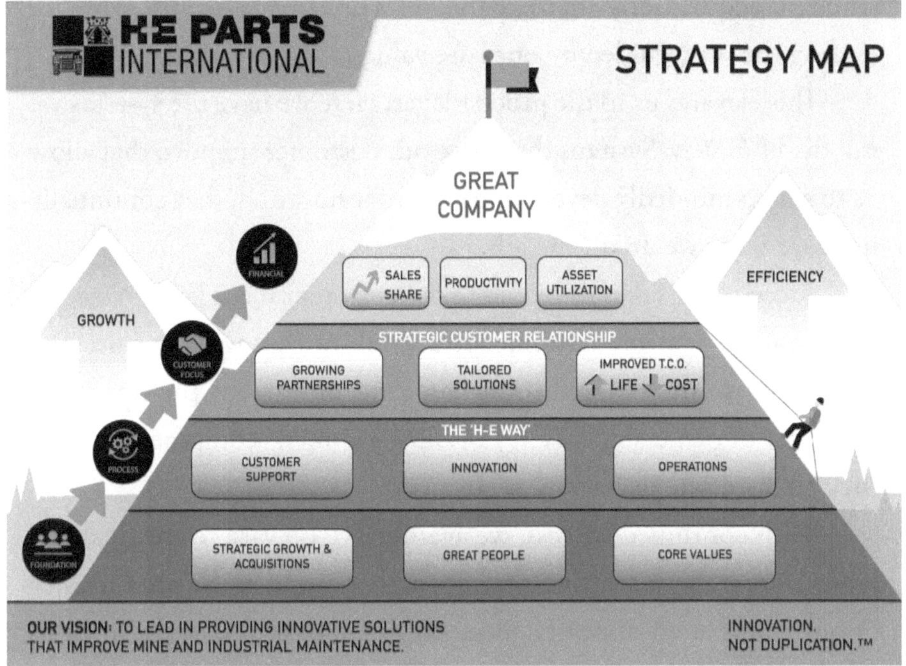

H-E Parts International—Updated Strategy Map 2018 (2020 Vision Campaign)

The principles driving this Strategy Map follow Kaplan and Norton's thesis, and specific measures will differ from company to company. What is important is that these measures are clearly communicated, understood by your teams, and offered with the expectation that every employee understands how they fit and contribute to the goals.

We distributed the Strategy Map throughout the company. It would be found in every common area and referenced in all global communications.

At the onset, we held meetings at every facility to introduce our Strategy, beginning at the bottom of the pyramid with a foundation layer to build on. For us, the foundation enables us to grow through strategic acquisitions that expand on our current teams, who are leading the way, guided by our core values.

This elevates us to the process layer. Here we have the systems we call the H-E Way. Systems that drive our customer support, that allow us to single-mindedly devote ourselves to innovation, that continually improve what we do on the job.

Success here takes us higher to the customer focus layer. Now, we focus on the strategic customer relationships that we'll pursue. The partnerships. The tailored solutions. And ultimately, the improved total cost of ownership (TCO) of our customers' equipment so that they gladly invite us back year after year.

With continued success, we again move upward to the financial layer. Here we seek to drive our sales higher, increase the productivity of our teams at all of our facilities, and put all of our assets to work as efficiently as we can.

Succeeding here takes us to the peak where we become known as a great company. Our Strategy Map has guided us to this summit. A worthwhile goal, accomplished.

This is the speech in summary, and then we'd go into breakout sessions with relevant teams. More on these in later chapters. Suffice it for now, this introduction was given at all of our facilities in seven countries. We referred to it regularly and equated our successes, new customer wins, and expanding product lines to the Strategy Map. Every promotion was tied, in some way, to the Strategy Map.

Our aim had to be global and commonly understood by all employees.

Our teams' multicultural, multicontinental ability to execute on this strategy map resulted in a company named Hitachi Construction Machinery purchasing H-E Parts for $240 million, representing a strong return and future success for H-E Parts International.

Critical to this success was a clear strategy, consistently communicated and backed by constant encouragement for employees to engage with the strategy and make it their own.

Turning Around Troubled Companies: The Manitex Story

If H-E Parts was a study in knitting various acquisitions together into a cohesive, productive industry leader in a multicultural world, Manitex was initially the opposite.

Manitex International began as a spin-off from Manitowoc. The company was acquired and listed on Nasdaq by its former CEO and chairman, David Langevin. I knew Manitex well. They provided mobile truck cranes, industrial lifting solutions, and aerial work platforms in a $110 billion market that overlapped in places with H-E Parts.

Manitex had acquired and divested several companies, and its investors rightly saw Manitex as an underperforming business. But I believed there was hidden value in Manitex. The company had unusually loyal and positive customers. It also had a very talented and committed middle management team.

This meant the Manitex management team could, like Ted Lasso learning to coach soccer in the UK, bring an open curiosity to the prospects before it, suspend judgment, and be humble, teachable, and open-minded. In so doing, the company might be given enough of an allowance from shareholders to attempt some novel turnaround maneuvers.

It wasn't certain, but it was worth a try.

Manitex had all the necessary ingredients to thrive—great people, great products, and customers who genuinely appreciated the company. What was missing was a breakout plan that everyone could embrace and execute on together.

So we ran a bottom-to-top assessment of the company with the goal of developing a strategy that we as a team could believe in, along with a Strategy Map to guide our way forward. In this assessment, we identified what appeared to be the three root causes of the company's underperformance:

LACK OF COHESIVE STRATEGY

- Businesses had been acquired but then allowed to operate independently.
- Major divisions in the company were being neglected, practically disowned.
- Units in the European theater and the US theater felt no need to cooperate.
- The company's many strengths were not being fully leveraged.

It was not the most flattering assessment, and yet few in the company would disagree with it. That was good, because it meant we could drum up internal support for change.

LACK OF BRAND IDENTITY

Since Manitex had grown swiftly through acquisitions that were never adequately integrated into a cohesive whole, the brand was all over the place. Customers and employees alike were confused about what the company stood for.

In my first two months with the company, I traveled to our key locations and met with our top customers. One customer summed it up concisely: "We like Manitex; its products and its people. We just want to see the business thrive."

So we undertook a rebranding initiative. Here's the graphic illustration that we shared with company employees and investors—the before and after …

Manitex Rebranding (2022/23), part of Elevating Excellence

As you can see, we took all the existing brands and gave them a common look and feel, similar to business deal tombstones or deal toys known to signify success. And we narrowed the multiple brands down to five, all under the parent company banner of *Elevating Excellence*. This rebranding, we hoped, would clearly communicate Manitex's new long-term value creation strategy.

Our future would thus depend on our acting as one team with one overarching mission to "elevate excellence" in our industry.

LACK OF AN ONGOING SCORECARD

In an industrial business like Manitex, only about 10 percent of the employees will have advanced degrees. Many haven't finished high school, or come from stable families, or enjoyed the amenities of modern life. Yet these individuals are the core workforce. It's a non-trivial task, therefore, to communicate strategy to them in a way that resonates when, frankly, *resonates* is not a word they will ever utter.

You have to show how their daily tasks fit into the company's grand strategy, and how the strategy's very success depends on the tasks before them. To do this, they need a scorecard that they can understand and take pride in, and they need to know how important it is to the operation.

That had not happened previously at Manitex.

Folks who worked in the service department were never going to understand or care about operating return on investment or internal rate of return. But to now discover that their delivery efficiency went from 82 percent to 93 percent in the last quarter—that's meaningful, doubly so when actual customers were brought in to view that scorecard as well, and to meet and shake hands with the people who had improved on those crucial metrics.

And to see the look in our service team's eyes! Practically beaming, standing taller. They were being seen by the customer. They were being praised by management. Their department was making a difference.

That's communicating. That's gaining buy-in, or as I put it to the team, "Order fulfillment up seven points this quarter! Couldn't be prouder. Okay, now let's talk about how we'll make next quarter's numbers even better."

This is executing on the balanced scorecard.

FIGURING OUT THE TURNAROUND STRATEGY

Our competitors were four to twelve times the size of Manitex and strong performers at that. Vertically integrated. Stronger buying power. Offering more products. If we tried to beat them on their field of play, we'd lose. So we played to our strengths. We could be more agile. We could be more entrepreneurial. We could be more innovative. We could focus more intently on our customers. So we crafted a strategy to do just that.

1. Committing to a high-performance service-first culture
2. Deepening the intensity of our customer relationships
3. Offering a full suite of portfolio products/services
4. Putting quality and innovation first

In talking about this strategy with the team, I told them that it all boiled down to having a compelling vision of who we are and who we want to be. This vision could be as simple as:

Elevating excellence by giving full liberty to our teams to treat our customers with unsurpassed care.

Not just providing excellent products, but making a difference in the lives of our customers, our employees, and our investors.

Delivering practical innovations and equipment that ratchet up the quality of our construction and maintenance processes.

The key would be uniting around this vision and making it the basis of teamwork. Too often, companies herald their commitment to teams but not to teamwork. But it's not one or two standout individuals in the organization who elevate excellence; it's diverse teams united by the core values we've all agreed to.

So yes, these core values would embody who we are as individuals and as a company of individuals. They would instruct us on the expectations we have for each other and for our business. They would reflect a culture that is uniquely Manitex.

To ensure that every employee fully grasped these core values, we communicated them in a graphic they could all relate to.

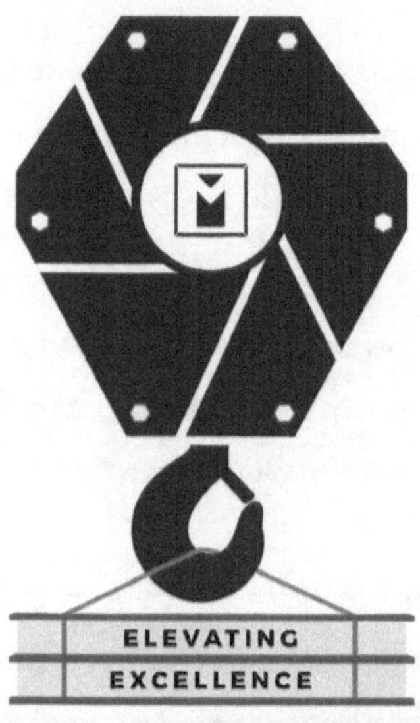

EXCELLENCE

Professionals committed to delivering quality results in everything we do.

CUSTOMER FOCUS

In everything we do, our focus remains on the customer.

TEAMWORK

We are unified in purpose & collaborative in action & respectful in every situation.

INTEGRITY

Safely doing the right thing.

ACCOUNTABILITY

We are pro-active, taking an ownership mentality in all we do.

DEDICATION

We are passionate & resolved in our work.

INNOVATION

We are curious, willing to learn & creative in our solutions.

EXECUTING THE TURNAROUND STRATEGY

And we executed as follows:

Step 1. Establish a common identity for all Manitex properties—a single modern logo, giving Manitex a "one team, one mission" look and feel.

Step 2. Write and dedicate to a Strategy Map that brings out the best in our Manitex culture by embodying our core values of customer focus, teamwork, integrity, accountability, dedication, and innovation. Here's the summary graphic of the strategy map we shared with the team:

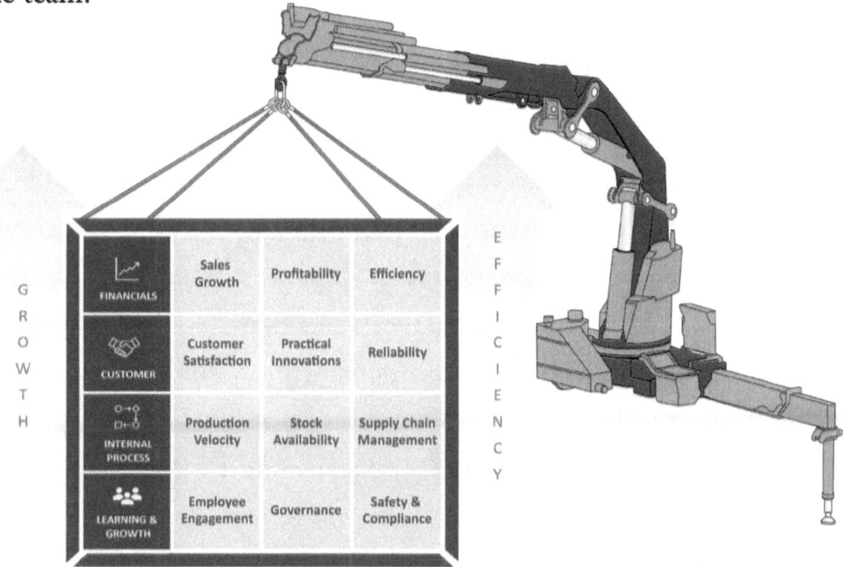

ELEVATING EXCELLENCE BALANCED SCORECARD

Step 3. Communicate our aspirational goal as a team. We aimed to grow our capacity and output by 30 percent and improve our operating profitability by six points.

Step 4. Execute on the plan and measure for accountability.

Summing up, Elevating Excellence was devised to help us succeed against much larger competitors. The strategy had to be global by design but executed locally to be successful.

Our board was presented with their version of this plan to comprehensively improve our competitive positioning, offer clear motivational direction to the team, and leverage our global account capabilities via a balanced scorecard. The board approved.

With both H-E Parts and Manitex, I found myself communicating that our strategy was centralized, but our success and execution would be decentralized. Our strategy was global, but its implementation had to be local.

RESULTS OF THE STRATEGY

Elevating Excellence, our three-year plan to revitalize the business, increased sales 38 percent to $297 million while improving EBITDA contributions by more than 400 percent. These turnaround results were sufficient to prompt a sale to Japanese crane manufacturer Tadano Ltd. In a definitive merger agreement, Tadano paid $223 million for the business, a 52.2 percent premium over Manitex's closing share price.

Objectives exceeded, a successful exit. And I was out of a job …

Origins of the **G.A.L.E. Force**

I was raised by a single mother who somehow managed to be the breadwinner, the homemaker, and the steady emotional center of our household—all at once. As a child, I didn't have language for what she was doing. I only knew that the system worked because we relied on each other. There was no redundancy. No safety net. If one of us dropped the ball, the whole thing wobbled.

That interdependence shaped me early.

For single parents, summers are not a season of leisure; they are a logistical gauntlet. School is out, childcare is expensive, and time off is scarce. My mother solved that challenge the only way she ever did—by finding opportunity where others might have seen constraint. She found a summer sailing program at the Rochester Yacht Club, and somehow, I won a scholarship that made it possible for me to attend.

For three summers, until I was thirteen, Lake Ontario became my classroom.

I still remember the smell of sun-warmed fiberglass, the slap of halyards against aluminum masts in the morning breeze, and the way the dock creaked under our sneakers as we carried boats down to the water. I remember the chill of early mornings on the lake, fingers numb as we wrestled stiff lines, and the quiet pride of rigging a boat correctly without being told.

At the time, I thought of it simply as freedom.

What I didn't yet know was how deeply sailing would imprint itself on the way I would later come to understand leadership, strategy, and execution.

The program taught us the basics of boating—how to handle lines, understand fundamental sailing principles, and practice safe behavior on the water. All of that mattered, of course. But what captured me completely were the racing classes. The competition. The clock. The flags snapping overhead as the start sequence counted down.

The instructors grouped us into teams of three, and once every third race, one of us would take a turn as skipper. When it was my turn, I took it seriously—probably too seriously. Most of the kids were there to have fun. I was there to win.

Looking back, I was almost certainly the annoying one—the kid constantly asking why we chose that line, why we tacked there, why we didn't press harder when the wind shifted. But even then, something about racing unlocked a way of thinking that felt instinctive to me.

Sailboat racing is, at its core, a live-fire exercise in strategy.

The course is set by the prevailing wind, but the path to each mark is anything but straight. You cannot sail directly into the wind. To make progress upwind, you must tack back and forth, constantly choosing angles, making tradeoffs, and adjusting in real time as conditions change. The winning boat is rarely the one that sails the shortest distance. It's the one that reads the wind best.

You win by choosing the right course, choosing the right sails, trimming them precisely, and coordinating your crew so that every small adjustment compounds into speed. Nothing happens in isolation. Every decision interacts with the environment.

That lesson stayed with me.

Years later, I would find myself transfixed by what may be the most demanding endurance race on the planet—the Vendée Globe. It's a sporting event few people have heard of, yet it represents the outer edge of human self-reliance and strategic execution. More humans have been to space than have competed in this event.

The Vendée Globe is a solo, non-stop, around-the-world yacht race sailed in sixty-foot monohulls. No crew. No outside assistance. No stopping. Just one sailor, one boat, and roughly twenty-four thousand nautical miles of the planet's most unforgiving oceans.

Skippers attempting "the Vendée" know they are committing to seventy to one hundred days at sea, circumnavigating the globe via the southern oceans, rounding the great capes, and sleeping—if you can call it that—in twenty-minute increments. Sometimes even less, especially when threading through ice fields in the southern latitudes. Every sailor is entirely self-reliant, constantly managing the risk of equipment failure, weather miscalculation, or physical exhaustion.

Modern satellite communications and drone photography now allow us to watch these sailors in real time as they build and revise complex strategic plans—gauging weather systems ahead, managing boats capable of sustained speeds of twenty-five to thirty miles per hour, and making thousands of solo decisions that determine whether they remain competitive or slowly fall out of contention.

Miss a weather pattern, choose the wrong route, or fail to adapt quickly enough, and you don't just lose ground, you lose the race.

Those images, those lessons, were very much on my mind in early 2025, as I wrapped up the business exit negotiations that handed Manitex over to Tadano. Once again, I found myself out of a job with something I hadn't had in years: time to think.

I began reflecting on how closely sailing mirrors the challenge of running a company in today's global, multicultural environment.

Earlier in my career, particularly in executive-suite roles, I had understood that articulating company strategy rested squarely on my shoulders. Like many leaders of my generation, I looked to history for guidance and found a consistent message: the most successful global companies were built on highly centralized strategies. Decisions flowed from the top. Alignment was enforced. Consistency was king.

And so, like many others, I followed the trend. After all, as the saying goes, the trend is your friend. But over time, in my work at H-E Parts and later Manitex, that assumption began to crack.

The global mining companies we served were, in many ways, centralized at the top and deeply decentralized at the bottom. Barrick Mining Corporation, for example, had its executive leadership team headquartered in Toronto, but its mines dotted the continents. While a global infrastructure and governance flowed from headquarters, real operational decisions were made on the ground, in the pits, shift by shift.

The decisions made at a mine outside Perth were often very different from those made in Wyoming. Different labor markets. Different regulations. Different cultures. Different constraints. Local finesse wasn't optional; it was essential.

As a supplier of mission-critical components to the heavy equipment those mines relied on, it became clear that our own success depended on mirroring that same operating logic. A one-size-fits-all strategy imposed from afar would never work. We had to align globally while executing locally.

When I finally had the space to step back and put a framework around what we were doing instinctively, it simplified into a phrase that felt almost obvious in hindsight: Global Aim, Local Execution.

Over time, it shortened to G.A.L.E., since the metaphor fit perfectly. Like a sailor out on the water—whether crossing a harbor or circumnavigating the globe—success depends on trimming the sails to harness the local winds and convert them into forward momentum toward a global destination.

A company doesn't cross oceans by wishing for wind. It crosses them by capturing the wind where it sails. It must navigate shifting weather systems. It must rig itself with sails designed to convert energy into speed. It must trust its crew to adjust constantly, intelligently, and in alignment with the broader course. That is the **G.A.L.E. Force** in action.

The **G.A.L.E. Force** charts a global course along the longitudes of strategy and scale, while relying on the latitudes of local insight and execution. Its destination is shaped—and accelerated—by the unique currents of each market it encounters. By tapping into the strengths of local cultures rather than fighting them, the organization harnesses a powerful gale force that drives global ambition forward.

A summary view of the **G.A.L.E. Force** looks like this:

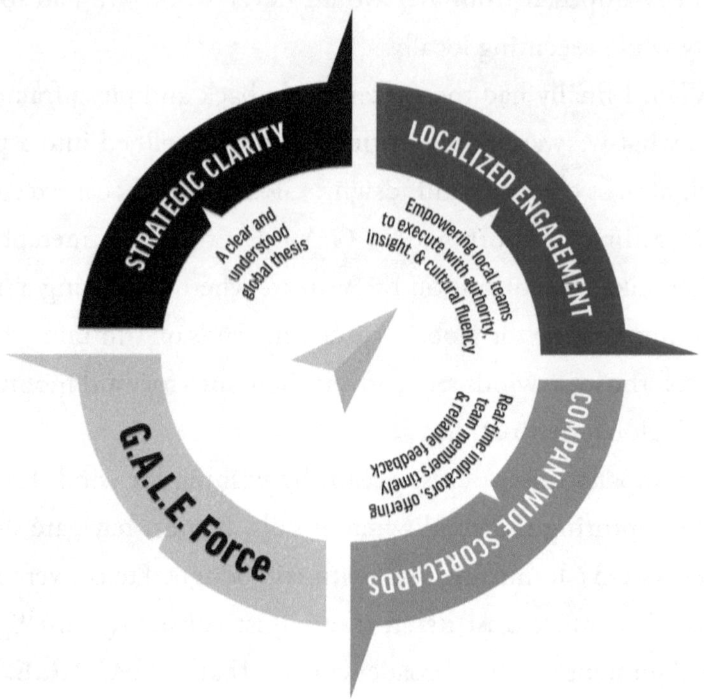

G.A.L.E. Force—*Global Aim, Local Execution*

Strategic clarity. A clearly articulated global ambition, supported by shared priorities, capital discipline, and infrastructure that enables scale without suffocating local initiative.

Localized engagement. Local teams that are culturally fluent and granted decision-making authority to align with local cultures and execute to meet on-the-ground realities.

Companywide scorecards. Simple, transparent performance measures so every team member knows how they're progressing toward shared goals.

We'll return to the **G.A.L.E. Force** repeatedly in the chapters ahead. But as with any voyage worth taking, it makes sense to begin by understanding the winds we're sailing in—starting with the powerful, and often underestimated, crosswinds of corporate culture.

Weighting Culture to Your Strategic Advantage

As a frequent flyer who logs more miles than the average Delta pilot, and an early riser, I revel in stepping into a city just as it awakens. Every place has its own way of shaking off the night. Some unfurl slowly like a curtain drawn back, while others snap to life with a full-throated roar. In those first fragile minutes between dark and daylight, you can feel how wildly different cultural touchstones can be from one stop to the next.

Modena, Italy, is quiet in the mornings. Small cafés stand ready for the commuting Italians dropping in for an espresso on the walk or drive to work. The mornings are not reserved for lingering. Espresso is purchased, drunk at the counter, and then people are off to work. It is in the evenings and especially the weekends when the city springs to life in its timeless allure. Long reunions attract family and friends in the Piazza, while children run free in the square.

In Santiago, the mornings are relaxed, and conversations tend to be soft and courteous—belying a fierce national pride that doesn't advertise itself, but is there. I've even joked that if there is an available square meter, someone will paint a Chilean flag there.

Perth awakens to the white-hot Australian light at a slower pace. Bicyclists and runners abound in the morning along the sun-struck Swan River before you see the shopkeepers. And when the cafés open, they fill with people who can talk mining royalties, footy results, and global affairs with equal fluency. There's an ease to Australians that can fool outsiders into thinking the culture is casual. It isn't. It is simply confident.

And then there are bracing mornings in Billings, where the Montana air can taste like sage and dust, and the first people you'll meet are headed to work in boots. Folks will look you in the eye longer, measure you a little more carefully, and once satisfied, speak to you with a directness that can be disarming if you're not used to it.

In these early morning walks, I learn much more than any market report could reveal. I ask everyone I meet about their city, their politics, their schools, their views on the US, anything they'll share. The conversations are interesting, personal, and illuminating. They reveal what is unique about the local culture, its essence, and what is immutable.

Culture doesn't care to bend to visiting executives and their latest schemes. And yet it is the substrate on which a business strategy must find footing, or quietly fail. So yes, it is only foolishly ignored.

Only by Immersing in the Culture

I learned about unbending culture the hard way.

As mentioned, I was due to arrive in our Chilean offices for a full week of scheduled meetings, including a critical one with BHP Escondida—the largest miner in Chile. I was excited about the prospects and had prepared with our local team for weeks. But when I arrived at BHP's Antofagasta headquarters, it was nearly empty. Everyone was off watching the Chilean soccer team at the Copa finals. Two days prior, Chile had advanced to the semifinals against Peru. The weight of soccer (fútbol to them) in the culture dwarfed any responsibilities the locals had to our company. It was one big kick in the pants.

So in the aftermath of that failed visit, I had a choice.

I could fight to have my way, or I could figure out how to use the local culture to our company's advantage. It wasn't the hardest of decisions, really. I knew well that happier employees tend to perform better. So the next time the Chilean soccer team was successful at the COPA, we scheduled a big barbecue, bused in all the families and invited customers, cleared out the shop, and put up a big screen to watch the game and celebrate together. It became an event, a very positive one.

And as approaches to management go, it is fair to say it dropped wonderfully to the bottom line. During that period of time, 2016 to 2020, we doubled the size of a business that had been growing in only the high single digits. It came from a two-part process:

1. Figure out what motivated our employees.
2. Build those motivations into the cultural fabric of the company.

Of course, even despite its size, a Copa final is not a full expression of local cultural priorities. Culture is an inch-wide-and-a-mile-deep kind of thing. Trying to define it is tough, and so often it leaves you spouting stereotypes or banalities. But if your goal is to harness culture into a genuine management advantage, you have to look past the comforting generalities and into its moving parts. Culture is not a slogan or a mood; it is a machinery.

And every market on Earth has tuned that machinery a little differently.

I sometimes picture culture as a great wooden wheel with unique spokes. Each of these spokes carries the load of those things we call culture. Stories people tell about themselves. Unspoken rules and norms that everyone knows. The idioms and humor that make their language sing. The rituals that quietly structure their days. All of the things that people call home.

These spokes are all essential elements of the local culture, giving it structure and durability and generational momentum as well, as skills and apprenticeships are passed down through generations from parent to child.

All of these elements of a cultural wheel have to be well studied by an outsider coming into the local culture, for they may not be overtly recognized and cannot be taken for granted.

By respecting this culture wheel, a company can ride along on its momentum. Trying to oppose the direction of local culture may get you crushed beneath its undeniable trend.

This is the cultural imperative that a company enters into when it acquires a local business. Nations, regions, cities, and yes, companies, have unique cultures. And it is naive to imagine you can build something that lasts without paying reverent attention to the wheel of local culture steadily turning beneath your feet.

By looking closely at the wheel's spokes—their heft, their history, their nonnegotiable importance—you are treating culture not as scenery but as terrain. You are then ready to build along the grain of a place, rather than accidentally carving against it.

Back in the classic era of globalization, a merger or acquisition in whatever country typically meant assimilation: making the acquired unit conform to the parent's systems and norms. In today's multicultural era, an M&A deal means *translation*. This process of translation is not some kind of passive adaptation but rather an active process of meaning-making. It asks, "How can our global systems express themselves authentically in this local language, this local rhythm?"

The best acquirers become translators that bridge global efficiency and local meaning. They build bilingual organizations, metaphorically and very literally, as well. They measure success not only in financial synergies but in cultural fluency. Such as with …

A Strategy Growing Out of Aikido

It is one thing to picture and appreciate this idea of culture as a localized wheel ever rolling forward. It is quite another to know how best to engage the wheel in motion. Operationally, that is the task of an executive: figuring out how to embed the company's nested culture within the rhythms and realities of the local culture. I was fortunate enough to gain deeper insights into this question from Ishii-san.

It was shortly after HCM acquired H-E Parts that our teams began reporting to HCM's senior vice president of mining, Sonosuke Ishii. I spent many hours with Ishii-san, and our conversations about Japanese culture were endlessly fascinating. Among these, Ishii-san shared his study of and devotion to aikido. He insisted that it kept him physically balanced, mentally sharp, and deeply appreciative of Japanese history, as well.

Aikido—*ai* (合), the harmony or blending of *ki* (気), the animating spirit, with *dō* (道), the way or path—is a martial art grounded in the principle that true power comes not from resisting force but from redirecting it. The practitioner meets an opponent's energy, aligns with it, and channels it toward a constructive end. This aikido, then, is an apt metaphor for navigating business across cultures.

When you recognize the forces in play and move with them rather than against them, culture itself becomes a strategic lever. You are leveraging the weight and momentum of culture—not by clever workarounds or circumventing local reality, but by understanding, respecting, and aligning with it.

We saw as much in Chile when we turned a local obsession with soccer into a regular celebration with our team and their families, drawing us all closer. By harnessing that local enthusiasm rather than resisting it, we strengthened our employees' and the community's trust in us. It would appear a small example, but far from it. For we captured the local cultural energy and turned it to our collective advantage.

Similarly, in Chile we would also celebrate Mother's and Father's Day—something I had not seen at any other company. It was a brilliant reminder of why our employees work, the deepest connections within our lives, and a reflection of the way family plays a deep and abiding role within the Chilean culture.

In a World of Culture Clashes

Like most Americans, I grew up in a culture that boasted of rugged individualism. I saw the world in terms of good and bad, innocent and guilty—a binary lens through which personal responsibility and individual choice were clarified. This dualistic worldview and focus on the self as the ultimate agent of action framed nearly every decision and moral judgment that US executives made for decades on the world stage.

Had I grown up in the Middle East or Eastern Europe, I would have internalized a culture of honor and shame. There, social perceptions outweigh individual judgment. Success and failure are measured not only by personal action but by how one's family, community, or tribe is reflected in that action. Reputation is currency, loyalty is sacred, and transgression is strictly punished. This is a collective-honor framework in which relationships and community standing shape behavior as fundamentally as laws or rules.

Had I instead grown up in Japan, I would have absorbed a culture of group responsibility and harmony. In this context, the individual acts in service of the whole—whether that's the team, the company, or broader society. Decisions are rarely about personal gain; they are about maintaining cohesion, honoring hierarchy, and avoiding disruption. Mistakes are not just individual failings, but they dishonor the group. This is the interdependent-group framework in which individuals are defined through their contribution to the collective stability rather than for any autonomous actions they may take.

Understanding these cultural differences and learning how to work productively within their constraints has become essential to doing business in a multicultural world. It is no longer enough to excel operationally or financially; success increasingly depends on one's ability to align strategy with the invisible, yet unyielding, currents of local cultural customs.

I've mentioned JP, the founder of H-E Parts, a couple of times. When we'd meet for our quarterly business reviews, an argument would often ensue. "Michael," JP would say, "so-and-so just said one thing, but you're saying another. Which one of you is lying? Who is wrong?" At first, I felt disrespected by this—like getting slapped across the face. Others, understandably, felt the same way.

But then a good friend who had lived in France for a decade explained to me, "Michael, in school in the US, if you were going to write a term paper, you'd be told to first outline all the positions you were going to explore and then open with an argument defending your best position, right? In the French educational system, you'd be told to explore all the positions and argue for *all* of those positions. A term paper in a French school is not complete until every position has been fully explored and argued for. If then you had a preference for one argument over another, at the end you would mention as much."

It dawned on me then. JP was arguing with me and getting my goat up because he wanted to make sure we'd fully explored all the positions. It was not an insult. JP was reverting to the culture of his youth to ensure we were making the best decisions.

EVERY CULTURE IS A LITTLE DIFFERENT

Most Americans think of Australians as jovial and easygoing, and they are, socially. But in business, they are regimented, organized, and very thoughtful in their pursuits.

Germans lean toward the pedantic, focusing on function and efficiency. From a design standpoint, Italians look for form as well as functionality.

For decades, northern Europe tended to look down disdainfully on the Italians because of their passionate manners. But truly, Northern Italy is quite industrious and adept at making even the mundane look great.

Recognizing regions of difference is critical.

Top Line of Global M&A

It now boils down to aligning a global operation with the local culture and using the influence, reliability, and attraction of that local culture to promote your strategic agenda. Some would call this cultural appropriation; they would be misinformed. In aligning with the local culture, your company is bringing out the best in the community.

Whether buyer or seller, there are going to be both strategic and cultural challenges.

Sellers must endeavor to articulate their strategy clearly, of course, but even more so, they must understand the buyer's strategic thesis. The sooner this is done, the sooner the value gap closes.

Buyers must endeavor to understand the strategy of the company being acquired, while also respecting its history and culture.

This weights culture to your advantage.

Culture—Formidable Foe or Valuable Ally

We have begun to see how culture, long a term that got little play at board meetings or in quarterly reports, can be a transformative term if understood in its fullest.

My own journey toward this thinking was far from a smooth one. In an early job in operations at Fluor, which provided major construction project support, I wasn't in a position to set corporate culture, and there were no recognizable core values guiding us. But as a division manager, I had leeway.

We had acquired a business with two union operations in California (Operating Engineers Local 3), and when we were formulating our 1998 fiscal plan, I held a "Members Meeting" every Friday for eight weeks. Attendance was voluntary, before work, unpaid. All but two of the union force attended. They'd been given a chance to weigh in on the business plan, and they did. They were invited into the strategy and encouraged to voice their thoughts about the company's direction. Though we couldn't measure such a thing, I was certain that this outreach effort made a difference in the quality of their work. There was something about having a say and being in the know that was attractive to these employees. Note to self.

When I moved on to Oldcastle in 2003, I was joining an industry leader in engineered building solutions. The CEO, Doug Black, challenged me to develop a strategy for my department and communicate it to our North American team. I was excited but daunted. Oldcastle operated as a matrix organization with employees often reporting to both functional department managers and project team managers. This style was great for collaborating, but it was often confusing with the dual reporting lines and all. Doug challenged me to articulate our strategy in a simple, memorable, and impactful way.

To try to bring some simplicity into a complex mix, as mentioned earlier, I introduced the simple "10 & 10 by 2010." We would improve utilization by 10 percent and decrease cost by 10 percent by 2010. The simplicity worked, and I would return to this trusty simplicity in later remits.

Aligning Culture and Strategy at H-E Parts with "PRACTISE"

As H-E Parts extended its global footprint—from engine remanufacturing centers in North America, to crushing rock operations in Australia, to service teams in Chile, Peru, Zambia, Canada, and beyond—it quickly became clear that technical integration alone would never be enough. We were not simply combining facilities, product lines, or balance sheets; we were merging distinct worlds. Each location had its own history, its own way of doing business, its own expectations of leadership and communication. What would make us successful in Wyoming would absolutely not be the same thing that created trust in Antofagasta or Brisbane or Lima.

We didn't have the luxury of monoculture. Mining doesn't work that way. Every site, every region, every crew, every supplier, every client brings its own cultural geology with its own shifting fault lines and tectonic plates of mindset and behavior that were decades in forming. If we didn't have a unifying philosophy strong enough to wrap around all that, the business would run like an engine with loose bolts. Everything rattling.

So in 2018, we sought to create a cultural operating system (a nested culture) that could be intuitive enough for teams of engineers, machinists, welders, rebuild specialists, and field technicians so they wouldn't see it as corporate wallpaper but as a tool they could use.

That system became PRACTISE: a set of core values arranged visually as a gearbox with an outer ring of seven values driving an inner ring of four. The metaphor felt right in a business that rebuilt four-hundred-ton haul-truck engines and kept twenty-four-hour mine sites running. People who work around big iron understand gears. They understand torque transfer, alignment, and binding. They know what happens when one tooth shears off. So we built a language that matched the lives our people were living.

PRACTISE became our means of translating culture into a durable competitive advantage. It gave our teams a shared constant—something universal—in an organization shaped by a multinational workforce, diverse acquired-company cultures, dozens of technical disciplines, and widely differing workplace expectations.

When we faced new integrations, market expansion, or entry into the cultural fabric of a new country, PRACTISE provided a common language for navigating the frictions that inevitably arise.

PRACTISE did more than articulate our ideals. It provided a global management framework. These principles both supported our strategy and informed our policy and decision-making. PRACTISE described H-E Parts' nested culture and better knit the company together through behavior.

- ✓ **Perseverance** built trust in slow, relationship-driven industries.
- ✓ **Responsiveness** made us relevant in fast-moving operational contexts.
- ✓ **Accountability** and integrity protected our consistency across borders.
- ✓ **Communication** prevented drift and strengthened cross-cultural clarity.
- ✓ **Teachability** and teamwork enabled integration after acquisitions.
- ✓ **Innovation** kept us uniquely customer-focused and future-ready.
- ✓ **Safety** created a universal expectation of heightened camaraderie.
- ✓ **Excellence** aligned personal development with organizational performance.

PRACTISE became the gearbox that allowed our multicultural organization to turn in one direction. It turned values into execution. It turned strategy into behavior. It turned cultural diversity into a competitive advantage.

And that is the larger lesson: Values are not soft. When constructed deliberately, they are the strongest hard assets a company has. They outlast leadership. They transcend borders. They bind together businesses that were not born together.

Values are the hard edge that yields a competitive advantage.

In the M&A context that most growing businesses are in, the practice of the PRACTISE core values makes the difference between a company that merely acquires and a company that integrates, grows, and thrives in a multicultural world.

Let's highlight three of PRACTISE's core values to see how these directly supported the strategy, while offering guidance to local leadership and local decisions.

RESPONSIVENESS—MAKING YOUR COMPANY INDISPENSABLE

Our aim was to deliver innovative solutions. H-E Parts was competing against much larger, more established businesses. We would never out-resource our competition. But we could out-maneuver them. This required a responsive approach to both our customers and our teams. If we could respond quicker and in a more fulsome way, we could close the value gap for our customers.

Responsiveness is an outward expression of an inner commitment. A customer-first mentality meant being responsive to needs. In some locales, responsiveness meant fast answers. In others, it meant thoughtful answers. In still others, it meant being physically present. What mattered was not uniformity but intentionality.

Responsiveness takes you beyond vendor to partner.

Mine operators live in a pressure cooker that tries to explode daily—commodity prices, equipment availability, regulatory shifts, political environments, and weather. When everything is unpredictable, the predictable partner wins.

So at H-E Parts, we sought to understand these pressure points and even anticipate them when we could. Across a global business, this required intense internal discipline, with systems that moved information cleanly across time zones, escalation paths that didn't break, and an organizational mindset that considered customer time more valuable than our own.

Responsiveness became one of our clearest competitive differentiators because it showed customers we had the guts to jump into the pressure cooker with them and figure out how to hold on. It's a practice of cultural alignment. And it's how we earned trust in an industry where a number of suppliers can look the same on paper.

TEACHABILITY—THE BASIS OF TEAMWORK AND AN ANTIDOTE TO EGO

You can't grow a multicultural business without teachability. You need people who are willing to learn from other markets, other skill sets, other ways of working. That means fostering an inner humility with a bend toward discovery and learning.

When I think of teachability, like many, I think of John Wooden and his Pyramid of Success—a philosophy rooted not in stardom but in team spirit. Wooden didn't recruit "great players." He recruited players who made the team great.

I think H-E Parts succeeded for the same reason.

Whenever our Chilean, Australian, and Peruvian teams worked shoulder to shoulder at tradeshows; whenever Zambian engineers collaborated with North American and Australian colleagues during system integrations; whenever finance and IT synced processes across hemispheres; in each of those cases, it was the teams' teachability and their teamwork that turned potential friction into synergy. It kept egos from getting in the way of collaboration, which is essential to keeping customers satisfied.

In a multicultural world, teachability is not optional; it's oxygen.

INNOVATION—THE ENGINE OF LONG-TERM VALUE

Innovation sounds glamorous, but at H-E Parts, it often meant something simple: finding a better way to solve the problem right in front of you. It embodied a commitment to creativity. How could we solve a problem by bringing innovation to bear? That was the first and last question of every day on the job.

Whether in engineering design, safety, sourcing, or process improvements, innovation was everybody's job. It lived in our mission statement (*Innovation, Not Duplication*) and in the way we encouraged every employee to contribute ideas that could improve reliability, safety, or cost performance.

Innovation wasn't a department; it was a daily habit, as natural as tying your shoe. And that mattered across the multicultural landscape we operated in. It gave our teams a shared north star that transcended geography. It also helped us maintain differentiation in an aftermarket crowded with competitors trying to imitate far more often than innovate.

Continuing the Set of Winning, Culturally Aligning Core Values

When taking the reins of Manitex after H-E Parts, I naturally began at once to define the core values of Manitex that would align our company with the cultures we operated in. This time, though, it was not a top-down exercise as it had been at H-E Parts. Manitex had a preexisting history, and I was the newcomer. Therefore, we asked the people who actually lived the culture every day to tell us who we were.

We commissioned a survey that started with two simple questions:

1. If you had to describe the company you work for, what adjectives would you use?
2. And when you think about this company in the community, why does it matter?

We didn't give our employees a list of corporate buzzwords to choose from, which would just box them in. Instead, we asked them to boil their answers down to one or two words. We did this in whatever the local language was—Romanian, Italian, Spanish, French, English.

The survey was not comprehensively given. Rather, we surveyed long-standing employees who had a history with the company. These were the employees who were considered the most knowledgeable about the markets in Italy, Argentina, and the US. What came back was revealing. Our Italian employees said "passion." So did the teams in Chile. Of course they did. Italian and Spanish are romantic languages. But we also knew we couldn't go around, as a multinational public company, proclaiming *passion* as our corporate virtue. Someone might get the wrong idea—we weren't looking to kiss anyone.

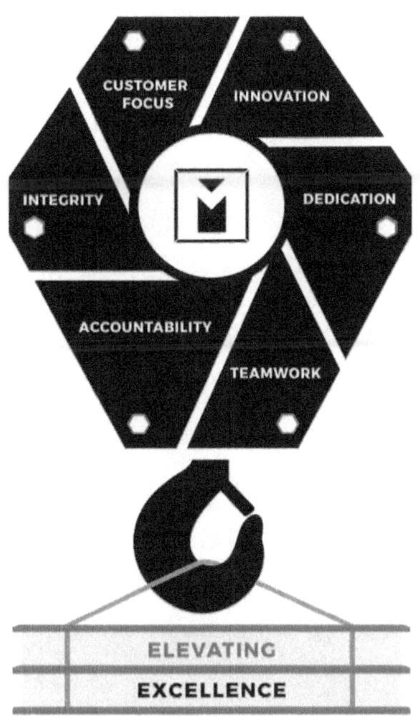

So our management team did get involved a bit, changing *passion*

to *dedication*. It captured the same fire, without the HR complications. And importantly, it was an exercise in framing a culture within a culture. The Manitex core values turned out to be different from those of H-E Parts. For Manitex, the overarching slogan was Elevating Excellence, and we highlighted seven core values to support it.

These seven values were meant to guide our business decisions, support our strategy, and be the foundation of who we were as a company.

When we did performance appraisals, we based them on an employee's adherence to those seven core values. Hiring decisions and promotions were made using these values. We communicated these values throughout the company, in monthly townhalls and in global quarterly newsletters.

Manitex had been underperforming prior to my arrival, partly because of its siloed nature. The company was not leveraging its strengths adequately, contributing to its underperformance. The slogan *Elevating Excellence* and the seven core values gave every employee at the company a common language, purpose, and identity—a nested culture.

With the core values becoming well-known and accepted at the company, we launched the *Elevating Excellence* awards. The awards were meant to recognize the seven individuals globally who embodied our seven values on a day-to-day basis. In devising the awards, we didn't have managers make the decisions. We had employees put forward the names of their peers. Managers and the executive committee had to then review these nominations, of course, but the lead belonged to the people who worked shoulder to shoulder.

Manitex Chilean and Argentinian team celebrate Elevating Excellence Awards. Left to right: Pablo Mesa, Michael Coffey, Cristian Pino, Matthia Iacoviello, Maritza Orrego, and Antonio Pagliula

I recall attending our awards banquet at Manitex's Chilean offices. Banquet is the wrong word—it was a barbecue we were hosting. All the local families were there, as well as employees flown in from around the world. The venue was packed, the employees all excited and yet nervous—these were no small rewards.

When I announced that the top recipient was a shop employee from the Chilean operations, the room erupted. People cheering, crying, hugging. Not because the employee had won—though that certainly mattered—but because everyone knew he was the *right* choice. Their choice. I knew we had honored the right person.

Had we chosen poorly—had the executives met behind closed doors and handed the award to someone who didn't live and breathe our values—the employees would have known it instantly, and the damage to trust would have been real. But by letting them lead, we strengthened the company in ways no balance sheet can fully capture.

Some might think a company's awards banquet is a small thing in a CEO's world. But when done right, it becomes something else entirely: a stitch in the untearable fabric of a nested culture. Later, after the dust had settled, one of the managers said, "I never thought we could win. I never thought we would be recognized."

It's all about doing the right thing by your employees, which has the added virtue of weighting the local culture to the company's strategic advantage.

Who Wants to Watch a Game Without a Scoreboard?

Rewind to the summer of 1904. The Olympic Games in St. Louis brought us a handful of firsts. The debut of gold, silver, and bronze medals. The welcome addition of women to the competition. And the most raucous, chaotic spectacle in athletic history, perfectly encapsulated by the marathon event.

This was no clean sprint. The course was a grueling 24.85 miles of dusty, rutted roads, where runners battled not only the distance but also the choking dust kicked up by passing cars and horse-drawn carts. In a truly baffling decision, organizers designed it as a scientific experiment in dehydration, placing only two poorly marked water stations along the entire track.

The result was total organizational failure.

The first runner back into the stadium—Fred Lorz—was nearly crowned champion before officials noticed he'd hitched a ride for much of the route. The actual winner, Thomas Hicks, had to be half-carried across the finish line after his handlers dosed him with a cocktail of raw egg whites, brandy, and strychnine sulfate in a desperate attempt to keep him upright.

The finish line was pandemonium. Officials bickered over rules, coaches disputed results, and medics tended to runners collapsing in the heat or searching for others who had simply wandered disoriented into the Missouri countryside. Spectators were left utterly bewildered—they had no idea who had won, which rules were applied, or what the scores even stood for.

It was an absurd, disastrous slice of history. And today, it feels uncomfortably familiar in the high-stakes world of business. Far too many companies are running their own marathons of mayhem: operating with murky rules, inconsistent oversight, and scoreboards that can't be trusted. When nothing is clear, nothing matters. And that is a recipe for corporate dehydration and collapse.

That chaotic scene from 1904 is not so different from the environment I encountered on my first visit to Georgetown, Texas, the US-based manufacturing hub for Manitex's truck-mounted cranes.

Corporate Dehydration Isn't Always Obvious

When I arrived, Manitex appeared to be a solid, publicly traded entity. It had acquired several brands during its history and had strong, market-validated products. However, the lagging stock price suggested that systemic issues needed addressing. And I was there to address them—to ratchet up Manitex's bottom-line performance and then target strategic acquisitions to add to the company portfolio. This was my mandate: to figure it out.

My first step was to convene the Georgetown-based team—comprising both front-line employees and supervisory management—to try to gain some insight into their operations. I put some basic questions to them ...

- How many cranes are you going to produce this month?
- What are your safety protocols, and your OSHA recordable rates for this year?
- How do you measure and maintain quality?
- What is your parts fulfillment ratio for the fiscal year?

Simple questions. Core business questions. None of them could be answered. Not by anyone on the site. Nobody knew what their budget was, or how many cranes were due to be completed that month, or how they were performing against expectations. Measures were gathered at the end of the month, but goals were not set or communicated to the team.

It was the 1904 Olympics marathon all over again. It was as if Manitex's employees were running a race, but the route wasn't marked, and there was no scoreboard. Nobody on that site in Georgetown had any idea of what success looked like.

If they had been properly in the loop, they would have known that they were supposed to build between thirty-eight and forty-two cranes that month. That was the correct number; somebody in the front office in Bridgeview, Illinois, was certainly aware of it. But the people building the cranes—from the supervisors and mechanics to the fabricators and operators—didn't have a clue. So when they clocked out each day, they went home not really knowing if they were succeeding.

The ramifications were serious.

I talked with the local Manitex team quite a lot on subsequent visits. Talked to them about *what it's like* to be an employee who matters. *How it feels* to be empowered to get things done and meet strategic objectives. *Why it matters* that you own your objectives and know you're driving in the right direction. *Where to go* in the company for support in better executing their part of the strategy. And *when to speak up* and say, "I'm not sure we're doing this right; I think we should try another way … and I have another way in mind."

Who gets the most excited and feels the most pride bubbling up inside when these questions are asked and answered?

It's not a hard question; we know that. When employees get a handle on the meaningfulness of their contribution in the bigger scheme of things, a very gratifying cascade of events usually follows …

Engagement levels go way up. People care more about their work. The team's overall work product improves. The company delivers on the KPIs you've set. All from lighting up a scoreboard for all to see!

I contend that no one wants to come to work to be insignificant. Given the opportunity, people want to have meaningful work. They want to know that their efforts matter, and they want to understand how their contributions fit into the broader goals.

Prior to Manitex, I had experienced a very different kind of disconnect that comes from different scorekeeping styles and cultures.

Colliding Cultures: HCM Acquires H-E Parts

When we put H-E Parts International on the market in 2016, Hitachi Construction Machinery Co. was one of the three finalists bidding for our business. Two others were private equity firms; HCM was a strategic buyer and very purposeful in their aims. They arrived at our corporate offices in Atlanta to run through items on their due diligence checklist. There were fourteen executives in near-matching suits, and they got right into their questioning.

Could we introduce them to our chief counsel, they asked. Our COO, CFO, and I all raised our hands, saying we did legal things too.

Could we introduce them to the IT director, they asked. Our CFO raised his hand, since he did double duty.

We took them to the server room—a closet down the hall where we also kept our snacks. Clearly, we were still in lean start-up mode and knew our compliance efforts could use some polishing up.

Despite looking like a scrappy start-up, we had truly prepared for going on the market. An acquisition spree that merged fourteen companies onto our platform meant some fast-moving and untidy handling of IP documentation. But we then backfilled fast and got pedantic about document custody and protection. We wanted all our ducks in a row in anticipation of selling the business at a handsome multiple.

So by the time HCM's fourteen suits combed through our files, our IP documentation and manuals were thorough. As a Japan-based company, HCM was ever fearful of doing the wrong thing. They checked everything.

In the end, they were satisfied enough to acquire us. They were getting our entrepreneurial flair—*check!* Getting our compounded growth of 7 percent a year—*check!* Getting an answer to their keenest curiosity: how our engineers had patented a solution to a long-standing brake and bearings issue that had plagued one of Komatsu's best-selling trucks.

That answer took us back to a single-week period when we discovered that one customer in Peru and another in Wyoming had the same nature problem on their trucks. It was a front axle assembly problem in both situations. We immediately surveyed our customer base and found that this problem was widespread across the globe. So we put our engineers to work at one of the problem sites—collaborating with the customer to figure out the problem, reverse engineering a solution combining proprietary H-E Parts' technology and the lessons we'd learned working on other trucks in the past, testing out the solution on one truck, then two trucks, then entire fleets of trucks around the world—while at the same time obtaining a patent on our design process.

To HCM, our innovative approach to the problem was the biggest *check!*

At the time that these HCM diligence meetings were going on, H-E Parts had seven-hundred-plus employees worldwide, but only seven in our corporate office in Atlanta. HCM was plain gobsmacked that so few people could run a company of our size. Their chief strategy officer and I had dinner after close, and he confessed, "We were confused by the size of your corporate office; how could you run such a company with only seven people?" I told him it was because our horsepower was in the field where our customers were.

We were decentralizing executables.

This decentralized design meant we had to have supercompetent people on the ground at sites around the world who could own the strategy and execute on it with some degree of autonomy in their local markets.

> *(This was the first execution of the* **G.A.L.E. Force** *multiplier I would later codify. I had often told our management team at H-E Parts that our strategy was global and fully vetted by the executive committee. But the execution on it—the way in which we would attain our goals—was decentralized. We*

offered latitude to local leadership, and we sought to empower them as much as possible.)

So HCM was happy with the nimble, responsive, localized approach of H-E Parts. But in joining HCM, we'd be merging into a culture known for its centralized governance and methodical decision-making style.

We were about to find out if two very different cultures could coexist.

When we agreed on terms with HCM, we were convinced it was a big win all around. And as time would pass, HCM would prove to be a great owner and do an exceptional job. To this day, I remain in touch with the leadership of HCM. But the cultural rub at the outset of our "marriage" was non-trivial, and would only become more so as time passed.

Despite having run the most exacting and excruciating diligence on us, HCM's executives did not fully think through the ramifications of acquiring a company whose revenues were fully dependent on providing solutions to OEMs' lines of business. OEMs that were, importantly, HCM'S competitors. This stood to cause problems for HCM—though we wouldn't learn why for several years to come.

WHEN AN ACQUIRER DOESN'T MAKE ANY CHANGES

At the time, we knew only that HCM (a) liked our strategy, (b) wanted our exposure to the equipment parts aftermarket, (c) were impressed by our numbers, and (d) said they didn't want to change a thing about us.

It seemed odd to us, but they didn't intend to make changes or integrate our business with theirs. They didn't even want to change our colors. HCM's big equipment was orange, but ours remained yellow. They allowed us to operate nearly autonomously.

The only real change, which we knew we needed, was the uncomfortably heavy blanket of compliance, risk aversion, and governance they wrapped around us. It did slow us down a bit, but we figured it was the price of playing in the big leagues.

We also knew, or thought we knew, that HCM's hands-off approach would someday, probably someday soon, come to a screeching halt. Why else would they buy us, we figured, if they didn't have a bigger plan in mind for us?

In M&A, an acquirer is never going to have a *fully* developed strategic plan before closing. You can't know *everything* going in. But you've got to have a good strategic thesis that's more fleshed out than, "We want more revenue and profit." Because if that's all you want, you can easily buy a Spider on the S&P 500 and not have all the headaches.

But months passed. No change.

HCM and our team both appreciated that, together, we were stronger. H-E Parts now had a global partner more than thirty times our size, and well-capitalized. HCM could point to real improvements in its weighted average of aftermarket revenues, its overall operating margins, and its appeal to investors. Again, all valid financial reasons for doing a deal. But if a sweet set of metrics is the *only* reason for the acquisition, it's not enough. There ought to be more.

We knew as much.

In our own brief history, H-E Parts had acquired fourteen legal entities. As we've discussed, we judged acquisition candidates based on the five legs of a stool. Having all five legs was always best, but three legs was the minimum acceptable level, and then only if our own company had strengths in the two missing legs. Those five legs were product complement, capability complement, scale potential, synergy potential, and financial health. Since this five-leg rationale had supported our global strategy, and because everyone in M&A used a similar version of this rationale, we just naturally figured HCM had something similar.

We continued thinking this well into the integration process. And the fact that, month after month, HCM remained quite hands-off only increased the mental energy we expended speculating about when the other shoe would drop. We were human, after all, and so we wondered: What the heck was HCM up to?

All we saw was an attentiveness and a keenness to study us and learn as much as possible from us. I would later consider this the most endearing quality of their management style. But at the time, given our own US-based view of the world, we read their keen study of us as a preamble to their doing something ("like a mad scientist playing with a bug on a microscope slide," was one of our team's half-joking theories).

Only as more months passed did it become clear that HCM was proving the exception to the rule that "everything will change." HCM didn't have a plan for us. It just wanted us to go on succeeding.

And frankly, that set us back, because it cost us the honeymoon period. In those first six to nine months after a merger, there is an opportunity to accomplish great things. But when the acquirer delays, a window of opportunity is lost. That's because, by our nature as humans, change is anathema to us, scary even. So when we're expecting it, that's when it will be easiest for us to go along with it, to give our support to it, to buck up and make it happen. But when we no longer expect change to come, and we grow accustomed to our new workmates, it's much harder to then change. We're dug in again.

In M&A, you have a magnitude of latitude within the first nine months. If that time is forfeited, any changes you need to make will require a whole lot more time, effort, and likely pain. With our H-E Parts team at HCM, we were about to learn that firsthand.

We had been operating in this state of corporate limbo for some time when our H-E Parts and HCM teams set out together to make the next HCM itachi acquisition, continuing the roll-up of the industry. We were targeting a small Australian business that had been on the radar for some time. It was a machining supplier that brought new capabilities, market expansion, a strong internal knowledge base, and was clearly a great fit. It's a deal that, in another time, our H-E Parts founder JP would have done in an afternoon. But with HCM, the process dragged on and on. The HCM's team's intense deference to issues of risk and compliance overrode their desire to complete the deal.

WHEN CULTURES REALLY DON'T SYNC

During this time, I gained even greater insight into HCM's approach to M&A. I was awed by their intense attention to detail and need to maintain control, but saw how different that was from the approach that had built H-E Parts. We had always known that the best mergers are going to involve companies of similar cultures, for they could go on marching forward in lockstep. But we also knew how rarely that happens. Indeed, over time at H-E Parts we had developed a strategy of leveraging the differences in cultures to the benefit of the combined companies.

The **G.A.L.E. Force** idea I was at the time developing would put our local leadership teams in charge of local operations, while back at corporate, we did our best to support them. Before HCM acquired us, we didn't have a single expat on the payroll in seven countries, by design. We hired the right local people who believed in our strategy. They helped author the strategy. They helped voice the strategy locally. They were accountable for making it happen. So the Chilean business was run by a Chilean. The Peruvian business was run by a Peruvian. The Australian businesses were run by Australians.

When HCM acquired us, it turned out that they had been outwardly impressed but silently distrustful of this decentralized structure of ours. It was a cultural thing for them, and nothing more. I decided to point out the obvious disconnect here at a big HCM strategy meeting one day, where I counted ninety-eight members of their global leadership team in the room. Only five of these ninety-eight leaders, one being me, were non-Japanese. To my amazement and HCM's credit, Kotaro Hirano, CEO of Hitachi Construction Machinery, solicited feedback in open session. Hirano-san had a natural curiosity and wanted to hear from us all. I was given the floor, and all eyes turned to me, attentive.

I asked why it was that HCM didn't have a single European leader in their European operations. By contrast, the American company Nike did not have a single American running its operations in France or Germany, but instead had a Frenchman and a German. The risk of trying to control these businesses from Japan, I continued, was that they could fail because the rules had changed. In a multicultural world, you can have a global strategy, but you're not going to change the local culture. An American business won't cotton to a Japanese management culture. A Chilean business is *no bueno* in the American management culture.

For example, I pointed out to the ninety-eight attentive faces that, in the old days, customers would call H-E Parts and we'd get to work on a problem within weeks and have it beta tested and improved in six to nine months. Other manufacturers might take years to fix the problem, or not even try. So our speed to market and the nimbleness in our culture have been a big differentiator for us.

But now HCM was being so tight with IP control that our H-E Parts teams had more access to HCM's competitors' details than we had to our own. Only the other day, I continued, my team had been asked for a remanufacturing solution on an HCM part. We wanted to gain insights from HCM, including manufactured drawings. So I went to HCM's IP librarian and asked for a copy of our original drawings. I was told that there's a compliance rule that restricts the sharing of those drawings with employees.

I recalled the conversation going something like this …

Me: We have been asked for a remanufacturing solution for this HCM part. Can you please send over our original drawings?

HCM: Can't do that.

Me: Okay, we are in the same company now, you know …

HCM: I am aware, but I can't do that.

Me: Well, you own 100 percent of H-E Parts, so you can do whatever you want. But without the drawings, my team can't easily design a solution.

In the end, we did manage to break the impasse, but these kinds of cultural restrictions definitely impeded our progress. It hindered our ability to be responsive—an H-E Parts core value. That became painfully apparent when, a few months later, we tried to leverage H-E Parts' global engineering and remanufacturing capabilities to expand remanufacturing in a key Caterpillar product area. Caterpillar was a competitor of HCM, and the component was fundamental to mining equipment propulsion and efficiency. It required dependence upon OEM parts and service records, in this case supplied by Caterpillar's dealer network.

During a self-audit, we became aware that we were accessing Caterpillar IP using software and internet connections common to the industry. We informed HCM legal of this, as well as our dependence upon this coordination of information. This opened the door to theoretical liability for HCM. The probabilities of actual liability were extremely low, but HCM was correct to fully explore this with us to ensure that we were not violating internal intellectual property (IP) policies or the law.

Although this issue had been investigated during diligence four years prior, the issue was raised to the highest levels.

We had run through our IP with them, how we developed it, how we managed it, everything. Diligence had revealed that barely 3 percent of our revenues came from work we did on HCM machinery, whereas 95 percent of H-E Parts' revenues were directly tied to products and solutions designed for Caterpillar, Komatsu, Metso, and Sandvik. So again, HCM could be concerned that we might be using IP or trade secrets that were not our own.

We understood these concerns.

That's why, back before HCM had acquired us, we put in place policies about possession and ownership of data and verified written use rights for data and designs that were not ours. What's more, going back to our formation, we tried to be careful with IP that was not developed within our own clean-room environment.

There had been times, years back, when a well-meaning customer or vendor would share a blueprint with us, tossing it onto the table and asking if we could make this or that. On a few occasions, this even became a point of contention because we simply could not accept external designs without a known chain of custody and authorization to use the intellectual property. This principle was in keeping with our vision of innovation, not duplication. We were in the solutions business, pure and simple, and we insisted on rigorous reverse engineering and internal solution development. Clients needed to allow us to develop our own designs, and they came to know it.

WHEN CULTURAL HURDLES CAN'T BE LEAPED

HCM soon encountered a cultural hurdle it had not fully anticipated. We proposed developing an IP-related component for one of HCM's competitors—something we had done successfully before—but the response was immediate and immovable. Senior legal counsel intervened, emphasizing strict compliance standards, and internal approvals slowed to a crawl.

What appeared on the surface to be a legal concern was, in reality, a deeper cultural hesitation. No one wanted to be the person responsible for taking a risk that might later be questioned, or for escalating an issue upward unnecessarily. As a result, decision-making stalled, and the project ground to a halt—not because it was unworkable, but because the organization was structurally unwilling to confront the possibility of being wrong.

We were being blocked from moving on an opportunity, despite HCM having known all along that 95 percent of our revenues were directly tied to products and solutions designed by other OEMs, despite our having demonstrated pristine handling of IP, our clean room environment, and strict document possession and custody standards. HCM knew all of this, yet it was now a huge sticking point.

This was four years into HCM's ownership, and the small gaps that had existed in our two cultures now looked like an uncrossable chasm. I was losing sleep in the Tokyo hotel room where I was spending too much time. I called my wife back in Atlanta, called other people I trusted, and sought their counsel. The next morning, I walked into HCM's offices and told the leadership we had done well;

the business and EBITDA were ahead of target, but it would be best if HCM found a new CEO of H-E Parts. It was time to move on.

We were not at odds. I treasured our friendship, in fact. It was a cultural issue that could not be resolved. I ended up working for HCM for another fifteen months, and I remained on the board for two and a half years after that. All very pleasant. To this day, I correspond regularly with HCM's CEO. We were both just doing our jobs, as we culturally understood them.

CONEXPO 2023. Left to right: S. Ishii, M. Coffey, K. Hirano, and N. Yamada

In defense of the Japanese way, it is what drove the nation's ascendency globally in the 1980s and 1990s. It was their devotion to total quality management (TQM). There's a beauty in the way they think. They do not think as individuals, by nature. They're very aware of who they are as individuals, and not above saving their own skin. But there's a higher order of thinking of the team. Back before laser-measured 3D computer-aided design and computer numerical control machining allowed you to spit out products accurate to a micron every time, you needed employees who would follow specific guidelines. Japanese culture enabled that. If you visited a US factory on the 4th of July, it would be empty. But visit a Japanese factory on National Foundation Day (commemorating the founding of Japan and its first emperor), and nobody would go home until quotas had been met. Completely different cultural ethos.

But of course, technology has marched on since the 1990s, and Japanese businesses operate at a relative disadvantage now. A clear lens on that came out of my travels with HCM's Senior Vice President of Mining, Sonosuke Ishii. He and I had become close, and we often traveled together. On one trip across North America, we stopped in eight major cities. Afterward, as I always do, I asked Ishii-san what he was seeing. "Mike-san," he told me, "in the US, every major city has a world company headquarters. In Seattle, we saw Boeing, Starbucks, Amazon, Blue Origin. In Minneapolis, we saw 3M. In Chicago, we saw McDonald's and United Airlines. In Japan, all major companies are headquartered in Tokyo—centralized in one location."

He was enumerating something deeply embedded in Japan's culture. Businesses in Japan are more centralized, a reflection of their aversion to risk.

In today's world, the risk control abetted by centralization is no longer a competitive advantage. TQM is less critical now. The operative differentiator is now collaboration and information exchange and speed to market. The new economy moves on transparent information exchange, nimble fluidity, speed, and flexibility. Japan's embedded honor-shame culture holds them back.

Our big takeaway from this is the importance in M&A of *aligning* cultures and *knowing* the scoreboard going in, and *recognizing* the difficulty in getting both of these right. Aligning, knowing, recognizing—it's a tall order. And indeed, it's what I like about the **G.A.L.E. Force** in action.

The **G.A.L.E. Force** (Global Aim, Local Execution) takes as a given that two cultures aren't going to align perfectly just because you want them to. Merging companies are going to have different histories, different personalities, different training, and different lots of things. It doesn't even matter if they're from the same city; if they have different starting points, one's family-owned and one's corporate, for instance, they're going to have different cultures, and they're not always going to align like you want them to.

What matters, then, is that you have a clear strategy for aligning the two merged entities at the local level where it matters. And then you overcommunicate your strategy to all the employees of both companies. This is done by finding things people can work on together effectively. That's where the core values bubble up and really, really matter. When both teams can agree on those core shared values, and can have scorecards in hand to measure the progress being made, then the two companies can (in time) align culturally.

Measuring Your Way to Success

There's no shortage of good management measurement tools out there, but few have had more staying power—or delivered more practical value—than the Balanced Scorecard, created in the early 1990s by Robert Kaplan and David Norton at Harvard Business School. They built it around a simple idea: If you only measure financial results, you'll only manage the past. But if you also measure the things that create those results—people, processes, customers, and learning—then you stand a chance of steering the organization toward a better future.

The Balanced Scorecard captures this cause-and-effect logic elegantly. It organizes performance into four perspectives—Financial, Customer, Internal Processes, and Learning and Growth—and shows how improvements in one area ripple into the next. Healthy companies use it not as a poster on the wall but as a living framework for improving efficiency, accelerating growth, and, of course, driving profits.

Importantly, the Balanced Scorecard turns strategy into technicolor. Strategy can now be seen by people, whether they have an MBA or not. The otherwise fuzzy concept of *execution* becomes a dashboard people can understand and rally around.

Now, the wrinkle.

When the scorecard becomes a top-down exercise, it rarely produces the same results as one built bottom-up. This is because executives tend to report what they think is happening, whereas employees default to telling you what is actually happening. And if the front line doesn't understand, believe in, or participate in the scorecard, you might as well be measuring the weather.

Which brings us to one very powerful bottom-up tool: the employee engagement survey.

THE SIMPLE VALUE OF EMPLOYEE ENGAGEMENT SURVEYS

In the early H-E Parts days, we did not have the resources or time to formally survey our employees. We simply weren't mature enough financially to run a meaningful survey process. Or if we did, we were far from prepared culturally to do something worthwhile with our findings.

HCM'S acquisition changed that. HCM was introducing a new tool to survey its employees, and their initial plan was to survey only the management team. Given the choice between surveying the executives and surveying the people who actually keep the wheels turning,

I'd pick the employees every time. So I asked HCM whether they'd object to including everyone we could reach.

Employee Engagement Surveys—Undervalued Tools

- Engagement surveys give employees a safe way to offer feedback, a way that protects them from feeling vulnerable. There will always be disagreements and tough patches among a team, but people can deal with that. If, however, they are not listened to, they will disengage, and then regaining their trust will be incredibly difficult (not skiing down Mt. Everest difficult, which some crazy guy just did for the first time, but hard enough).
- Whenever feedback is received—whether informally or through organized surveys—build it into an action plan with the objectives clearly shared with the team.
- Perform this action plan and report the results back to the teams. Make a show of the reporting.

Engaged employees are more likely to ...

- Feel they have a stake and a sense of accountability that only a business stakeholder can feel.
- Be more focused, happier, even healthier—all infectious things.
- Soon be introducing the company to family and friends, or posting online about the company on their own, at which point you're golden.

After explaining the whys and wherefores, we got the green light. We issued the survey to 430 of our 780 employees. That might look like an underwhelming ratio, but remember—we had folks working in remote locations, without email, without computers, and frankly without much appetite for anything resembling "corporate feedback." Even so, we achieved a 75 percent response rate, which we considered impressive.

Before we launched the survey, I gave the leadership team (our executive committee) one nonnegotiable. I told them, "If we do this survey and don't respond to what we learn, we'll be worse off than if we'd never done it. But if we listen to the responses and act on them to close the loop, our culture will get stronger. Not overnight, but certainly and steadily."

The first question one guy on our executive team asked was, "What if employees ask for something we can't give them?"

My answer: If our response is honest, it will strengthen the business. People can handle bad news and will accept "no" for an answer, as long as we are respectful and truly hear their point of view. Simply put, we talk about it with them. We explain our position. If we still disagree afterward, that's fine—we've shown that we value them. We've opened a door. We can return to that doorway. The act of honest conversation is itself a cultural win.

Once the survey was complete and the results compiled, we found that our teams had a seventy out of one hundred engagement score. Not terrible, not great. Average, in fact, with plenty of headroom. But here was the magic: Once this measurement mechanism existed, it became *real.* Employees knew the organization was paying attention, and they naturally began paying more attention too—improving on the things that they could, speaking up more, and taking pride in the scoreboard.

Three years later, our score hit ninety-two—squarely in the "excellent" zone—and we were outperforming every other HCM unit worldwide by twenty-five to thirty points. In a heavy industrial business, scores like that are almost unheard of.

Why the jump? I think there were two reasons.

First, we invited employees into the strategic process. We showed them the field, the end zones, and the scoreboard. We connected their daily tasks to the company's broader strategy, so work wasn't abstract anymore—it had meaning. When people understand how their actions matter, they lean in.

Second, the executive committee took full ownership of the results. We never shared anything personal or punitive. If someone wrote "Michael Coffey is an idiot," we didn't publish that (mercifully for me).

Instead, we published—and acted on—the data that mattered. We flew to every facility and held town halls. We shared what we learned, celebrated the wins, and built improvement plans together to address deficiencies. We created a feedback loop that let employees see the impact of their voices.

Bottom line: In a consumer products company, engagement scores like ours might raise eyebrows. In a global industrial business, they raise the roof. And it all stemmed from showing people how their daily actions linked directly to strategy—and giving them a scoreboard they could be proud of.

PUTTING SURVEY RESULTS TO WORK

Our survey evaluated fifty-six categories across operations, culture, communication, leadership, and organizational performance. The results were unambiguous: H-E Parts was a great place to work. Employees were proud of the company, proud of their teams, and deeply engaged in our success. Teamwork and mutual respect weren't slogans—they were visible, measurable realities.

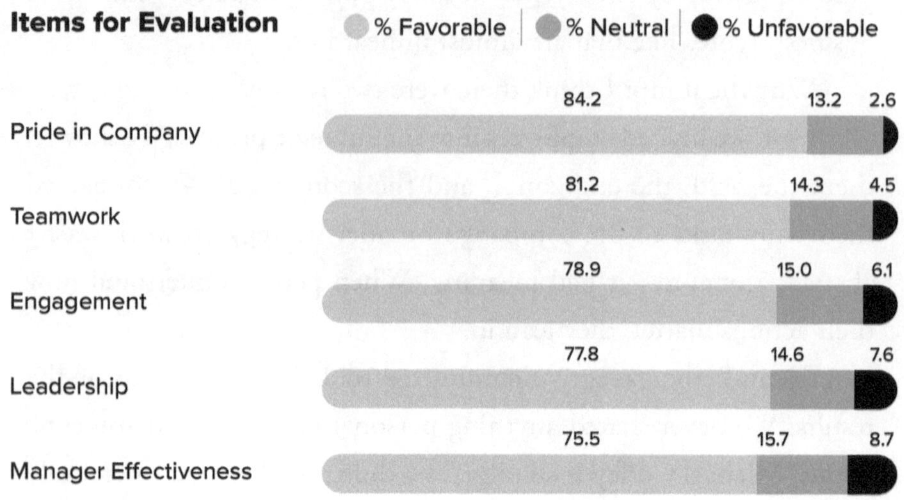

High satisfaction is wonderful, but only if it helps us locate the pressure points—the areas where we need to improve.

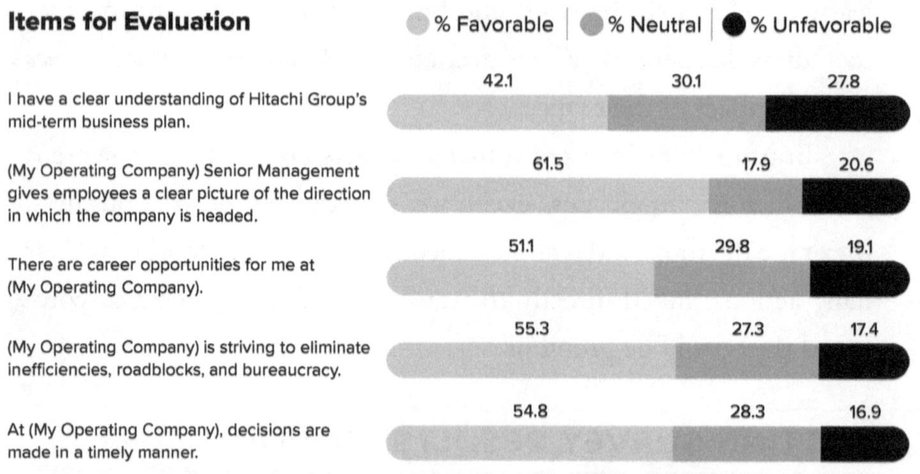

One of the biggest gaps was understandable: Employees didn't feel they understood HCM's midterm plan. Fair enough—we were still learning how to navigate our new corporate parent. But ignorance is never a strategy. People can't execute what they don't understand, so we put a priority rush label on overcommunication—choosing to err on the side of over rather than under.

Other findings included …

- a need for more direct and frequent communication,
- frustration with organizational siloing inside HCM, and
- a desire for more individual and team training.

From the entire exercise, our takeaways were clear:

- Running an annual engagement survey is a lot of work—but absolutely worth it.
- Seeing strengths and weaknesses through employees' eyes is essential for continuous improvement.
- When employees know the survey is safe and taken seriously, they naturally become more competitive and more collaborative.
- A well-run engagement survey becomes a powerful strategic accelerant. Employees stop being "the workforce" and start becoming co-architects of the company's future.

Constantly clarifying, measuring, and engaging—that's how you light up the crucial scoreboard of business success. Teams tend to disengage quickly when rules are unclear or when success metrics are withheld. At Manitex and H-E Parts, our use of transparent scoreboards and meaningful feedback mechanisms boosted performance and ultimately increased our exit multiples.

Tools such as balanced scorecards and surveys amplify the cultural system, giving employees visibility into how their work connects to strategy, and a genuine voice in shaping the organization. This is the practical side of culture, the side to be lived, measured, and reinforced.

Now, let's look at how hard this can be to carry through with!

The Soft Art of Leading Hard Things

Every company has its cape closet. No one talks about it, but everyone knows where it is. And sooner or later—during a crisis, a budget showdown, a missed quarter—the "superhero" reaches in, throws on the cape, and stands there in the double-teapot pose, bent arms with fisted hands at the waist. These people are conversant with their résumé, reciting it verbatim as they describe how they are going to save the day. Often, it's the CEO. Other times, it's the VP of Ops or even a regional manager who just knows that they were built for the superhero moment.

Once, during a turnaround situation, a regional GM proverbially climbed onto the conference table like he was Thor, hammer in hand, spinning tales of the past and telling his staff that he personally was going to "pull this turd out of the crapper." And he believed it.

But within five minutes of my own ball-peening around the office, it became obvious that the company's problem wasn't the product spec, or the latest marketing drop, or customer acceptance, or even some epic competitive struggle the company was engaged in. It was the GM's own warrior's honor. He was long on heroics and short on systems thinking.

This is often called the superhero fallacy, and we see it even in well-run companies. Someone decides that the fate of the free world rests squarely on their shoulders and they alone can fix whatever crisis is at hand. These caped crusaders just know that if they parse the numbers finely enough or tighten the bolt tightly enough, they'll single-handedly save the day. It's a seductive illusion. It puffs up the ego. It feels like leadership is being done.

And the thing is, these superheroes sometimes do save the day and then strut off into the sunset, with admirers aplenty. Surely guaranteeing that next time a crisis presents itself, you know who will ride to the rescue, hammer raised or guns blazing.

And damage intensifying.

Yes, damage intensifying. Because even in the movies, the superheroes may save the day, but when they fly off, all the after-action mopping-up work is left to someone else. And in companies, it's no different.

Genuine corporate performance, performance that is durable, repeatable, and bankable, rarely comes from a lone star. It comes from the unglamorous architecture of success: well-designed teams, clarity of process, aligned incentives, shared culture, and unfiltered flows of information.

Superheroes collapse under this kind of heavy complexity.

Companies today stretch across continents, cultures, jurisdictions, time zones, supply chains, and networks. There is simply too much happening for one person to "fly in" and grab the controls.

Perhaps the most damaging behavior of superheroes is their need to hoard information. Would-be heroes usually insist that all communications route through them. They believe they are adding value by filtering, curating, and managing the message. But they're not filtering reality, they're distorting it. They're protecting their comfort, not the organization's clarity. And without clarity, decision-making becomes guesswork dressed up as leadership.

To work toward clarity with senior management in my companies, I've found it helpful to insist on four rules of engagement:

With Managers, CEOs Reserve the Right to:

1. Call any employee at any time and ask any question they like directly.
2. Resist giving direct instructions to employees on the team—that's the manager's job.
3. Keep managers informed when engaging their teams without undermining local leadership.
4. Have firsthand touchpoints—with customers, employees, suppliers, everyone.

These four rules are simple enough to post up on the board, but difficult to adhere to—especially as the organization grows. But it is no secret that the larger the organization, the more important these rules are, because the more curated the CEO's reality becomes. And once CEOs are insulated, they hear only half of what's going on, and they don't know which half. Far from satisfactory.

These four rules can be traced back through the annals of leadership. One example of them comes from Robert E. Lee. While the general was on the indefensible side of history, the study of his command remains, to this day, enlightening. One of Lee's core principles was simple: Do your own reconnaissance. He didn't lead from the tent. He rode the field himself. He studied terrain, weather, distance, and soldier morale. He believed a leader must know the ground—meaning, see reality firsthand. This behavior may feel a bit primitive in our age of digital dashboards and metric-spewing machinery. But in reality, it's far from primitive.

Today, as ever, a filtered leader is a half-blind leader. And half-blind leaders are well positioned to make fully catastrophic decisions.

To build a culture where leaders can see clearly, you must create systems of respect, trust, and transparency—structures that allow leaders to move freely, listen freely, and learn freely. When people are *not* afraid of the truth, they share it. When leaders are *not* insulated from the truth by gatekeepers, they hear it. When teams are *not* dependent on superheroes, they become one another's support systems.

Organizations don't need capes. They need clarity. They need collaboration. They need systems so well-designed—and people so well-aligned—that no one has to be the hero in the first place.

For decades, senior leaders were expected to have all the answers. CEOs were expected to ask all the right questions, as though they had superpowers or intuition. Senior leaders today, especially in a company growing via M&A, need to be highly collaborative. If anything, collaboration is the modern superpower.

How Team-Builders Outperform Superhero Day-Savers

In the mythology of entrepreneurship, the spotlight often trains on the lone genius—the brilliant savant hunched over a workbench, the mad visionary who willed a contraption into existence by sheer force of personality. It's an attractive story because it simplifies success into a single face and one heroic arc. But when you strip away the romance and study the enterprises that have survived across generations and leadership changes, a different pattern emerges. The real engines of durable success are not superheroes who save the day from time to time. They are team architects who build the systems that hold up over time.

The day-savers produce heroics, great moments, and dependencies. The team-builders create momentum, systems and structures, and replaceability.

Herb Kelleher built Southwest Airlines on the conviction that if you take care of your employees, they will take care of your customers, and the numbers will take care of themselves.

Sam Walton wandered the aisles of his stores with the quiet intensity of a man who knew his success was borrowed from the people sweeping the floors and stocking the shelves.

Mary Kay Ash created an army of empowered sales leaders by giving them a platform to step higher on, not a pedestal to admire her from.

These founders didn't scale because they were uniquely brilliant, but because they designed environments where other people could win.

Many great businesses have thrived precisely because they had superheroes at the helm, bent on saving the day. Absolutely! But the odds are against them. Their superpowers will always be stretched thin if there isn't some semblance of teamwork backing them up.

Businesses that instead choose to build great teams are often the hardest to beat.

THE TWO ENTREPRENEURIAL CEOS		
	Team-Builders	Day-Savers
Primary Strength	Architect of culture, systems, talent	Personal brilliance, intuition, genius
Leadership Model	Delegates, develops, distributes	Centralizes decisions; personal execution
Decision-Making	Transparent sharing in context	Rapid top-down pronouncements
View of People	"We win when our people win."	"We win when I'm right."
Role of Culture	Strategic asset that's teachable	Often implicit, founder-dependent
Likely Outcome	Durable, transferable enterprise	High upside but fragile scaling
Great Examples	Sam Walton (Walmart) Herb Kelleher (Southwest Airlines) Howard Schultz (Starbucks) Mary Kay Ash (Mary Kay) Eiji Toyoda (Toyota) Konosuke Matsushita (Panasonic) Akio Morita (Sony) Soichiro Honda (Honda) Robert Bosch (Bosch Group)	Henry Ford (Ford) Ferdinand Porsche (Porsche) Thomas Edison (GE) Enzo Ferrari (Ferrari) Elon Musk (Tesla) James Dyson (Dyson) Steve Jobs (Apple) Bill Gates (Microsoft) Larry Ellison (Oracle)

Everyone Lauds Teamwork, Less So Teams

Every executive has proudly uttered the phrase, "We value teamwork!" Of course they have. But how many actually understand how to build a team that *wants* to win?

Leaders who understand know that it's less about issuing memos and posting mission statements, and more about building a nested culture of people united by a shared purpose, mutual respect, and measurable outcomes. At H-E Parts Chile, that meant a lot of singing and coffee and dirt and grime under our fingernails.

DEVELOPING AN H-E PARTS TEAM EMPOWERED TO WIN

When we held quarterly management meetings at H-E Parts in Santiago, the first half was devoted to the usual things: reporting, metrics, financial review, personal development. Our quarterly business reviews would be held with our regional leadership (a member of the executive committee) and their team. When business was over, we would enjoy dinner at a local restaurant. That was until Javier Carraminana offered to host dinner at his home. It was a brilliant idea, and I'm eternally grateful that Javier hosted dozens of these barbecues.

In time, we would select a menu and everyone would Uber to Javier's to cook together, enjoy Chilean wine, and, to my surprise, sing songs together. Any magic we created wasn't in the quality of the singing—especially not with my voice in the mix. It was in the shared experiences that bonded us together, and I have added to my repertoire "Puerto Montt" and "Gracia a la Vinda."

Francisco Li-Jo Lay, division controller, and Cesar Jonquet, general manager, preparing ceviche

H-E Parts Chilean leadership team.
Life lesson—a great way to build trust together is to cook together.

Each morning in Chilean culture begins with a leisurely cup of coffee. If I arrived at work eager to jump into my "to-do" list for the day, I'd set the team on edge. In that culture, the custom is to begin the day with a cup of coffee together and a catch-up conversation. It's what's expected, and it builds trust—the currency of effective teamwork.

Later in the day, the entire team—management, engineers, and technicians alike—might find ourselves under a Komatsu big haul truck trying to figure out why the dang thing wouldn't go. We were in the parts business, and we'd work hard to figure out the dirty, oily, greasy part that needed repairing, replacing, or remanufacturing—whatever was required to get that big, expensive truck going again. Sure, the engineers were in the lead, but when the entire team was there backing them up, we all felt a much greater pride in the work we were doing together.

The word *teamwork* is but a sterile slogan until it is turned into one shared memory after another, tying people into a community of shared values and interests, creating a nested culture that has value to every participant. That's the real stuff of teamwork.

At every work site, people want to do well. Want to contribute. Want to feel ownership over the work product. But it only happens when strong leaders open the door and invite team members to give their best, to put their skills to work, to feel pride in the outcome. Creating the safest possible space for the team to do their job, and then ensuring that each person's contribution is recognized—that's the job of a leader. It's a skill that requires empathy, attentiveness, and humility to be done right.

FROM ENGAGEMENT TO OWNERSHIP

In his book, *The Truth About Employee Engagement*, Patrick Lencioni cites three root causes for job misery: anonymity (feeling invisible or unknown), irrelevance (not understanding how one's work matters), and immeasurement (being unable to tell whether one is succeeding). As Lencioni puts it, "Every human being who works has to know that what they do matters to another human being." He describes this as the fundamental truth of employee engagement.

Those three negatives, he argues, are countered by three positive roots of genuine engagement.

The first is belonging—the feeling of being known. Truly engaged employees don't just show up; they act like owners. They are invested because they know they belong, and they know they matter. Leadership affirms it. Peers reinforce it. At work, they know their colleagues—and are known by them.

Why wouldn't a company invest deliberately in this sense of being known? The relationships we build at work are often the only things we carry with us when the job is done. I've been fortunate to develop lifelong friendships with colleagues around the world. I've met their spouses, watched their children grow up, and feel genuinely blessed to call them friends. That sense of belonging didn't just make the work more enjoyable—it made it meaningful.

The second root of engagement is meaningful work—being drawn into the why of work.

I learned this lesson the hard way. After a disastrous first semester in college, my mother arranged for me to work during winter break at a plastic injection molding plant. I wasn't a natural student, and my GPA made that painfully clear. My mother, with her signature directness, said, "I've seen your grades, and I've arranged for you to work to help fund your tuition. I'm not paying for this level of performance."

So off I went—ten hours a day standing in front of a molding machine, opening a door, pulling out a plastic part, closing the door, and repeating the cycle. I had no idea what I was making, how the machine worked, or why any of it mattered. The work was mechanical, disconnected, and joyless. But the lesson landed. I graduated with far better grades, fueled by a new understanding of effort, purpose, and consequence.

People want to be drawn into meaningful work. They long to understand not just what they are doing, but why it matters. Leaders can—and should—provide that context by clearly articulating the how, the why, and the impact of the work.

The third root of engagement is feedback.

Earlier, we noted that no one wants to watch a sporting event without a scoreboard. Work is no different. People deserve to know how they are doing. When they're performing well, good leaders tell them. When they're not, good leaders help them course-correct. Measurement, when done humanely, is not pressure—it's clarity. And clarity is one of the greatest gifts a leader can give.

MEETING EMPLOYEES WHERE THEY ARE

A recent analysis by Suzy Welch in *The Wall Street Journal* called attention to an apparently widening generational "values gap." While many companies have long treated some form of *achievement* as the ultimate metric, younger employees—particularly Gen Z—are fully convinced that the ultimate metrics in their business lives are *learning, care,* and *purpose.*

They are still young and idealistic, yes. But they want to see how their work matters, not just to the company, but to themselves, their communities, and the values they hold. This trend, which began with

Millennials, appears to be solidifying with Gen Z. And it appears to have sticking power—in one manifestation or another.

How does management meet this new generational ethos and *not* risk disengaged employees or disappointing rates of attrition?

I've found that meeting employees—of any generation—is not about coddling or lowering standards, but instead, it's about alignment. Leaders must clearly show how each person's contribution aligns with and, in fact, is deeply interconnected with the larger organizational mission and strategy. This means giving context for decisions, sharing outcomes beyond the individual's immediate tasks, and making visible the ripple effects of their work.

Beyond connection, leaders should actively uncover and cultivate employees' passions. This might mean pairing a junior engineer with a senior colleague whose expertise matches the employee's interest, creating cross-functional projects that let someone experiment with new skills, or simply carving out time for coaching conversations.

In a multicultural, multigenerational workforce, this is plainly not optional. Respecting cultural norms, generational expectations, and individual aspirations is a prerequisite for building trust, engagement, and cohesion. Leaders who understand and act on these dynamics create teams that are not just competent but motivated to perform at their very best.

Ultimately, meeting employees where they are means turning the old top-down lecture into a two-way conversation. No longer is the objective to try to control outputs. It is instead about shaping employees' experiences and cultivating their potential. The result?

A workforce that feels seen, valued, and empowered to contribute in ways that drive both individual satisfaction and organizational performance.

EMBEDDING VALUES, NOT JUST POLICIES

The nested localized business culture we've been talking about most clearly doesn't come from an email blast or a binder of policies. It comes from your core values as they are felt, lived, and constantly reinforced.

Policies tell people what they must do. Values tell them why they want to do it.

And in any organization operating across borders, languages, and business traditions, the core values become the connective tissue that makes the whole enterprise work.

At H-E Parts, I learned early that a nested culture couldn't be dictated from the boardroom (recall my showing up to an empty office during the Copa finals). So we learned to build the culture through participatory value-setting. We invited employees to join in defining what mattered to them, and how we would operate as we grew. When employees then saw themselves reflected in the values of the company, they didn't just sign off. They bought in. They protected the culture—wanted to protect it—because they felt responsible for it.

This bottom-up approach is harder, but it's stronger too. That said, it is only half the **G.A.L.E. Force** equation. A truly strong culture needs essential top-down guardrails—clear, nonnegotiable lines about what the organization will not tolerate.

Every culture has its red lines.

At the companies I've led, our red lines were consistently: disrespect, dishonesty, safety violations, manipulation, and silo-building. So we articulated these boundaries plainly and tried to live by them consistently. It gave our employees the confidence that our nested cultures were not some ideal we aspired to, but a discipline we lived by.

In a global enterprise—especially one navigating acquisitions and integrations of multiple microcultures—these core values become the operating system. They determine how decisions are made when headquarters is asleep, how teams collaborate across oceans, and how people behave in the moments that never make it into a policy manual. Values are what people fall back on when the world tilts, the deal closes, and everyone must suddenly find a new equilibrium.

Embedding values, not just enforcing policies, is how organizations gain resilience: the kind that shows up in performance and the ability to move as one—even when stretched across continents.

Ultimately, teamwork is much more than a slogan. It's a system: designed, nurtured, measured, and culturally grounded. A strong leader has to create the conditions for teams to succeed by embedding values in action steps rather than plaques hung on the wall, connecting every employee's work to purpose, and transforming a team into a multiplier of value.

All of which might lead an organization, or its board, to wonder: How do we go about identifying gifted men and women who are capable of this kind of executive leadership? One way is with DRiiVE.

Driving Outsized Performance with DRiiVE

This idea of DRiiVE was born in the quiet turbulence that followed my decision to step away as CEO of H-E Parts. I remained on the board, but the cadence had changed. I was no longer in the daily rhythm of decisions, people, and pressure that had defined my life for years. That dissonance created space—and with it, a need to reexamine what I truly believed about leadership.

At the time, my thinking was still orbiting the **G.A.L.E. Force**. I had come to see G.A.L.E. as a powerful management construct: a way of aligning global strategy with local execution, of unleashing bottom-up capability by respecting culture, context, and human motivation. G.A.L.E. explained how organizations move—how momentum is created inside complex, distributed systems.

But as I refined that idea, deeper questions surfaced:

- How is that gale force harnessed?
- How is the ship steered and not merely blown off course?
- What prevents it from becoming energy without aim?

A powerful gale wind could easily capsize the boat or run it aground—unless the right crew was on board. To be effective, we needed to identify and develop the right kind of leaders. Who would these be?

Eventually, the question distilled itself into something both simpler and harder: "What are the irreducible qualities of leadership that cannot be taught but must exist in the man or woman at the top of the organizational chart?"

I turned that question over again and again while on a solo sailing trip off the Florida panhandle. Out on the water, the metaphor sharpened. I thought about the lone genius of a captain steering by instinct, versus the team-builder with an entire crew managing sails, charts, and keel ballast together. A captain could at best point the way; a coordinated crew could weather any storm. Likewise, in scaling a business, success would come to the captain who could inspire the crew to lean the ship just enough, at just the right moment, to turn force into forward motion.

What kind of captain would that be?

It wouldn't be someone who just picked up skills in business school or workshops and memorized textbooks. It wouldn't be someone with deep technical competencies in the domain either. Both of these would be qualifications, sure. But they weren't the elemental traits that define a leader at their core. A better definition would be required.

And I believe that in those searching weeks, I arrived at that better definition with something I nicknamed DRiiVE. As an acronym, it captured the essence of executive excellence that should be the standard in the wildly electric world of mergers and acquisitions. These are the essential characteristics of leaders that cannot be taught but are instead prerequisites.

Finding them is the art of successful executive team building.

D—Drive

Leaders, by nature, are self-motivated. There is something about Monday mornings that excites them. Drive is more than energy. It is self-motivation that initiates and propels action. No road map, no prompting, no problem. Leaders with drive anticipate the road ahead, seize the opportunities there, and keep the momentum going even when uncertainties pop up. In M&A, drive is the engine that keeps integration on track, decisions sharp, and teams aligned with the overarching strategy. Drive is the relentless pursuit of progress—not for recognition's sake, but because inertia is simply unacceptable.

R—Restraint

Restraint is the invisible hand of effective leadership. It is the ability to pause, reflect, and evaluate before speaking and acting. Our grandparents called it temperance, or the quality of moderation and self-control.

This quality is marinated with wisdom's best friend, time. Restraint is discipline under pressure, timing over impulse, precision rather than reaction. In transactions where great sums of capital and hard-won reputations are both on the line, restraint prevents rash decisions, avoids unnecessary risks, and signals credibility to all deal partners.

I—Intelligence (IQ and EQ)

Intelligence has to be multidimensional, encompassing curiosity, problem-solving, and an insatiable desire to learn (IQ) with the capacity to understand oneself and others, to navigate complexity with empathy, and to respect cultural, generational, and geographic differences (EQ). In an M&A context, we see this in the synthesizing of information, reading the subtle cues in negotiation, and kid-gloving the often fragile dynamics that can make or break an integration.

I—Innovative

Being innovative begins with the questioning of assumptions and conventions and ends with the crafting of new ways forward. So many people spend their workdays avoiding risks, cleaning up their messes, shielding themselves from exposure. Innovators, on the other hand, make messes, sometimes big ones, seeking breakthroughs—sometimes succeeding. This is the mindset that transforms obstacles into assets and issues into advantages. Innovation in business combines a willingness to solve a problem with creativity.

V—Virtue

Of all the innate traits of a born leader, virtue must be foundational. It is integrity in every action, humility flowing from dawn to dusk. It is an unwavering commitment to doing what's right—sometimes when it is the hardest thing to do. Virtue anchors the organization in trust, and every stakeholder ultimately values it. In an M&A transaction, virtue engenders the necessary trust and keeps parties out of the courtroom. It maintains reputations and is the natural exercise that results in long-term value creation over short-term expediency.

E—Ego

Ego in DRiiVE is truly the team ego—the ability to channel the team's personal ambitions into collective success. Such leaders convey messages in "we" and speak of their team's success. Their reward is manifest in the success of others. It is meekness, humility paired with confidence, the willingness to learn, and the maturity to be challenged. All without compromising performance or organizational value. This translates into the team's achievements outweighing any individual accolades. The team-driven ego ultimately magnifies the greatness that all enjoy.

EXECUTING DRIIVE IN NORTHERN ITALY

I joined Manitex as an outsider and had to quickly assess the strength and depth of its executive leadership. On day one, there were six general managers; the business required three to operate effectively. We moved immediately to close that gap. In Italy, our choice was Giovanni Tacconi—a twenty-year veteran with deep international experience. Within ninety days, he was named managing director. It remains one of the better decisions I made.

In my early months, Giovanni and I traveled together frequently. I asked him what an American should understand about Northern Italy. He gestured, more than once, to history—to the fact that our Italian plant quite literally sat on the foundation stones of the Via Emilia, the Roman road laid in 187 BC that became the backbone of northern Italy. He spoke of centuries of invaders—the Huns, the Franks, the French, the Spanish, the Austrians—all drawn to the fertile corridor between Milan and Venice and to a passable east–west corridor that avoided the imposing Alps. These were not abstract stories. They lived in the land, and in Giovanni. History there is not something you study; it is something you inherit.

Embedded in Giovanni's storytelling was the larger lesson: Trust in this region is not easily given. A new American CEO would be met with understandable caution, and no amount of title or authority would shortcut that reality. Only time, consistency, and shared work would soften those apprehensions.

At the same time, Giovanni taught me that respect—especially among leaders—can be earned by advancing step by step, in genuine collaboration. He embodied a deeply Italian sense of collective responsibility: Success belonged to the group, and no one moved forward unless everyone did. He recognized that same instinct in others. It did not take long for mutual trust to form.

As a member of the executive team, Giovanni became one of my most trusted and reliable leaders. He embodied DRiiVE. Together, we made meaningful changes to the business—no small task in an operation whose roots stretched back sixty to eighty years. Progress came not through force or disruption but through shared purpose, patience, and respect for what had endured long before either of us arrived.

Elevating Excellence demanded three things at once: market expansion, a six-point improvement in margins, and a higher level of operational discipline—all within limited time and resources. We began where the leverage was greatest: the product line.

One of Manitex's legacy businesses carried twelve crane models spanning two to ten tons of lifting capacity. Our premise was straightforward: The market could be fully served with just four of those models, provided they were equipped with the right accessories. Rationalization, not proliferation, would be the path to growth.

Left to right: Roberto Chiesa, Michael Coffey, Alberto Ranzi, and Giovanni Tacconi

Any manufacturer knows, however, that sunsetting products is never easy. Models born in R&D become part of a company's DNA. Retiring eight of twelve platforms would test both judgment and resolve. Giovanni—with his DRiiVE—was exactly the right leader for the task.

He led his team through a rigorous assessment: identifying the true market opportunity, selecting which legacy products should remain, and innovating new solutions that made those four platforms more capable, less costly, and better aligned with future demand.

The result was a simpler, stronger portfolio—one that reduced duplicative inventory and vendors while allowing us to scale volume and expand margins.

This was **G.A.L.E. Force** in action: a clear global ambition met with exceptional local execution. It could not have been driven from a corporate office in the US. Only the Italian team, given the latitude to reshape operations on the ground, could have executed this level of change effectively.

Giovanni approached the work with deep respect for the history of the business and equal clarity about its future. With humility and credibility, he called his team toward a new way of working—one that increased production, lowered costs, and preserved what mattered most. Doing so amid post-COVID supply-chain disruptions made the achievement even more significant.

And the results spoke for themselves.

Under Giovanni's leadership, the Italian operation delivered two of its strongest years on record. Our plans were aggressive, yet the team exceeded budgeted forecasts. Most gratifying of all, they surpassed their bonus targets. For more than a decade, the operation had fallen short and earned no performance incentives. Giovanni led them to reverse that pattern—further validating both the strategy and the leadership required to execute it.

Giovanni's example shows why DRiiVE is not a theoretical exercise: It is a framework for action. Drive, Restraint, Intelligence, Innovation, Virtue, and team-driven Ego are the levers that transform teams from good to extraordinary, that turn integration challenges into growth opportunities, that convert potential into realized value.

So when evaluating leaders—before, during, and after a deal—look for DRiiVE in action. Measure it. Reinforce it. Celebrate it. Because the right leadership team is not just the enabler of strategy; it can be the multiplier of value, the bridge between aspiration and performance, and the difference between an acquisition that sputters and one that soars.

Preparing for the Sale of a Lifetime

I was still young—green, really—working my way through the management training program at American Equipment Company (AMECO) when called into my first acquisition. It was a buy-side deal for a family-owned agricultural machinery dealer in Mexico called MAPSA. AMECO wanted to expand its footprint and saw MAPSA as a perfect partner: multilocation, respected name, deep roots in the region. The vision was to combine the two companies into a kind of cross-border superdealer.

MAPSA's president, Adrian Del Paso, had flown north to negotiate the potential sale on behalf of his family. There were over a dozen family members who owned MAPSA. Each one had a stake in the business, and each one expected Adrian to deliver the very best payout for them. He carried that responsibility in his posture, in the way he read every clause twice, in the way he kept pausing to calculate what each decision meant back home.

MAPSA couldn't simply liquidate and split the proceeds. Family businesses rarely can. Too much of their wealth—and their identity—is tied up in the enterprise itself. Every decision Adrian made affected someone's retirement, someone's home, someone's standing at the family table.

My role in this was to evaluate every one of MAPSA's leases—make sure they were legal, approved, and buttoned up for closing day. On paper, it looked like clerical work. In reality, it was an introduction to the emotional weight that underlies any family-owned business sale.

And there I was, a young guy with a stack of leases in a language I barely spoke, trying to look like I belonged in the room. I had never negotiated a commercial lease in a foreign country, much less across multiple product lines and multiple locations. But I had to get every property on a common platform—terms clear, signatures ready, and no loose ends—so that when the wire hit, both sides knew exactly what they were buying and selling.

Working side by side with Adrian on this, I realized something: We were both pretending to be calmer than we felt. He was trying to bring home a win for his family. I was trying not to be the rookie who fumbled the ball at the goal line.

Even when both companies want the deal done, you can feel the tension that always hangs in an acquisition. Sellers wonder, "Will they value what we built?" Buyers wonder, "What are we not seeing?" Everyone, whether they admit it or not, has a moment of, "What if I'm making the wrong call?"

In this case, the call was right. The combined AMECO-MAPSA operation has now enjoyed more than two decades of success. But the experience taught me something foundational: A great sale doesn't begin in the conference room. It begins long before—with preparation. The most successful sellers I've worked with weren't lucky; they were ready. So let's look at what drives owners to the table today—and then what "being ready" really means.

What Is Driving Sellers in Today's Market?

Business owners don't sell because they're bored, duh. They sell because the world around them—or inside them—finally forces the question. And understanding these triggering forces is the first step in preparing for a high-value exit (instead of being dragged into a mediocre one).

LIFE HAPPENS

Most owners don't plan their sale—they react their way into it. Burnout sets in. Health changes. A spouse says, "Enough." Kids don't want the business. Or the owner simply hits a point where the weight of the job no longer matches the joy. When that moment arrives, the sale becomes emotional, stressful, and too often rushed. A reactive seller almost always leaves money on the table. A prepared seller doesn't.

NO INTERNAL SUCCESSOR

This is one of the quietest but most common triggers. Owners want to retire, but no one inside the business is ready—or willing—to take over. Without a next-generation leader, selling becomes the only path that preserves what the family has built. In the selling, ideally, a good number of the key employees will stay on. If they don't, if the company's leadership bench is weak, it can trim a lot of zeroes from the sale price. The value drops significantly because the buyer's risk rises.

MARKET TIMING AND OUT-OF-THE-BLUE OFFERS

Sometimes the trigger is external …

- A strategic buyer appears.
- A financial investor wants a platform.
- Industry multiples ratchet upward.
- A company's IP or processes suddenly make it attractive.

This is the inflection point that can be the difference between an ordinary exit and a generational one. But a company only benefits from good timing if the house is already in order.

DESIRE FOR LIQUIDITY OR DIVERSIFICATION

Founders often have 50–80 percent of their net worth tied up in the business. That's the very definition of concentration risk. Selling—or even partially selling—lets owners de-risk their financial life and convert sweat equity into actual equity. It's not greed. It's smart stewardship.

HITTING A STRATEGIC CEILING

This is the turning point that many owners don't talk about out loud.

They look at their prospects lucidly and realize that they may not have the capital, energy, or appetite to scale into it. But the right buyer may be able to blow through ceilings that the seller cannot. This doesn't diminish the seller; it simply acknowledges economic reality.

Can this seller's realization hurt the company's sale price?

Not if the business is presented properly. Buyers love a company with a strong foundation and a clear runway—they just need to see where their fuel can take it.

EXTERNAL DISRUPTION

New competitors, regulatory changes, supply shocks, or technology shifts can create enormous pressures. Some owners want to double down and fight; others prefer to exit while the business is still strong. Both paths are legitimate and need to be mapped out fully, so the owner can make the best choice with all the information at hand.

When Is the Company Ready to Sell?

If one thing is misjudged above all others by business owners, it is this: the real, market-tested value of their company. Not what they feel it's worth. Not what they've invested in it. Not what they need for retirement, or what their neighbor's business sold for. The only valuation that matters is the one a buyer will land on after peeling back every layer, validating every number, and stress-testing every assumption. And that process—diligence—does not care what the owner hopes is true.

So before business owners even think about their M&A prospects, they must do something many owners avoid for years: make an honest, unvarnished assessment of their business as it really is. Because the buyer will certainly be doing that.

And if that assessment reveals weaknesses (it always does), then the preparation begins—often months or years before a sale is launched. The work is not exotic. It's the same work any owner should be doing to build a world-class organization. But in the context of a sale, the stakes grow sharper. Value is either created or destroyed long before the first buyer ever enters the room.

So how does an owner know whether the company is truly ready for the sale of a lifetime?

Here are the elements buyers scrutinize—and the initiatives a seller must address in hopes of receiving top-of-market value.

CAN THE BUSINESS SURVIVE WITHOUT ITS STARS?

Many companies are powered by one or two superstars—the founder, a rainmaker, a technical genius—whose presence is essential to operations. To buyers, this is not a strength but a risk. If the business could quite easily collapse without that person, buyers get nervous. They know they're not acquiring a company; they're acquiring a dependency, which is a much lesser-valued thing. Countering this potential problem requires …

- Documenting every team member's responsibility.
- Reducing the founder's or CEO's centrality.
- Distributing decision-making deeper into the organization.
- Developing a leadership bench that's prepared to run the company first thing Monday morning after the close.

A transferable business is a valuable business.

IS THERE A CLEAR, COHERENT STRATEGY?

A surprising number of companies grow without ever articulating a clean strategic plan. They operate on instincts, habits, and market pull—but not on a documented, measurable strategy. Buyers notice this because they want to know …

- Where is the business going?
- How will it get there?
- What are the metrics?
- What stands in its way?
- How does it scale under new ownership?

Tools like strategy maps, scorecards, and performance dashboards signal discipline. They tell a buyer, "This company plans, executes, measures, and adjusts." Clarity becomes part of the value.

IS THE CULTURE HEALTHY, DOCUMENTED, AND TRANSFERABLE?

Culture is the softest asset—until it becomes the hardest problem in an acquisition. Buyers look for

- codified values actually practiced (not posters),
- consistent leadership behavior,
- high customer retention,
- high employee engagement metrics, and
- a team clearly nested around something larger than a paycheck.

A healthy culture lowers integration risk. A dysfunctional or leader-dependent culture increases it. One gets a premium; the other gets a discount.

ARE THE FINANCIALS CLEAN, ACCURATE, AND DEFENSIBLE?

This is obviously important since only a foolish buyer will tolerate messy books, unexplained margins, vague categories, phantom assets, or unreliable forecasts. To be ready for a sale, financials must be

- GAAP-compliant or equivalent,
- clearly broken down by product, customer, and geography,
- transparent about adjustments, and
- audit-ready.

Clean financials don't just make diligence easier—they increase the multiple. Dirty financials destroy confidence and value.

IS REVENUE OR SUPPLY TOO CONCENTRATED? CAN IT BE DIVERSIFIED?

If 40 percent of revenue comes from one customer—or one vendor supplies 70 percent of inventory—the buyer sees fragility. Concentration risk is the enemy of valuation. The remedy …

- Broaden the customer base.
- Diversify suppliers.
- Build in redundancies.
- Reduce single points of failure.

Even small improvements here can dramatically increase a buyer's appetite.

ARE SYSTEMS AND PROCESSES DOCUMENTED AND SCALABLE?

Potential buyers are not just looking at today's operation but tomorrow's growth potential. They want to see systems they can plug into, replicate, and expand. Value rises when …

- Processes are fully documented.
- Technology and equipment are modern and secure.
- Workflows are standardized.

- Training is consistent.
- Core operations can scale without heroics.

A company built on muscle memory is fragile. A company built on systems and processes within a nested culture is valuable.

ARE THERE ANY HIDDEN LANDMINES—LEGAL, COMPLIANCE, OR OPERATIONAL?

Nothing chills a buyer faster than discovering

- unresolved litigation,
- open tax questions,
- ambiguous IP ownership,
- regulatory uncertainties,
- unknown liabilities, or
- entangled real-estate or equipment ownership.

Cleaning these up pre-sale reduces friction and increases buyer trust. It also reduces the risk of *retrading* (a buyer lowering their offer late in the process).

DO THE OWNER'S VALUATION EXPECTATIONS MATCH MARKET REALITY?

One of the most common deal killers is emotional valuation. Owners often price the business not on its performance, but on their sweat equity, their retirement needs, their best year ever, or, all too often, an anecdote from another seller. Buyers don't care a wit about any of that. They price based on risk, return, comparables, and future potential.

Closing the gap between owner expectation and market reality is crucial—usually requiring a full valuation or banker-led assessment before the process begins.

IS THERE A PLAN FOR LEADERSHIP, CUSTOMERS, AND OPERATIONS POSTSALE?

Buyers know there will be enough uncontrollables postsale, so they want to control all they can at the time of closing. To help with this, the seller should thoughtfully prepare

- transition plans for leadership,
- communication plans for customers,
- continuity plans for suppliers, and
- integration plans for systems and culture.

Poor transitions leave a trail of anger and lost opportunity. Strong transitions are the exact opposite.

What Buyers Most Prize in a Seller, and Reward

Having now seen or participated in hundreds of deals, I've found that quite consistently, buyers will pay premiums for companies that have

- a clear, executable strategy,
- a strong leadership team that can run without the founder,
- a healthy nested culture,
- clean financials with consistent performance and momentum, and
- scalable systems with low concentration risk.

Buyers aren't buying history so much as trajectory. A company consistently performing in the right direction, with the right disciplines, looks like a rocket that just needs a larger fuel tank. That's what commands strong multiples.

Accelerating into the Exit Chute

Once the business is ready—and just as importantly, once you are ready—the entire game changes. You stop operating like an owner with your sleeves rolled up and start thinking, speaking, and moving like a seller. It's a gear shift you feel in your bones. One moment you're in the familiar rhythm of running the place, and the next you're leaning forward into what I call the "exit chute," and then *wham!* You're on a roller-coaster ride before you can even buckle the harness.

And it really is a roller coaster. Exhilarating in one stretch, intimidating in another, with long, frustrating straightaways where nothing seems to happen, right up until everything happens at once. Your phone won't stop buzzing, advisors are talking over each other, a buyer wants a midnight call, and suddenly your heart is in your throat because you've just inked the most consequential signature of your life.

But here's the truth: The exit chute isn't just a metaphor. It's a mental transition. A reorientation. You shift from running the day-to-day to positioning the business—its people, its systems, its story—for the very best possible outcome. You move from "How do we execute this quarter?" to "How do we present the value we've created over the years?"

You begin curating, not just operating; guiding, not just grinding. This shift can feel strange at first, even disorienting. But when you make it deliberately and embrace the ride rather than brace against it, you give yourself the steadiness, the clarity, and the confidence to navigate the twists with purpose. And that mindset, above all else, is what separates sellers who merely survive the transaction from those who maximize it.

Let's break down how this unfolds …

DEVELOPING A STRATEGY YOU CAN LIVE WITH

Everything begins with understanding why you're selling and what success looks like. Clarity here sets the tone for the entire process.

For some, success is purely financial: Maximize the price. For others, it's about preserving culture, protecting long-tenured employees, or keeping the company's mission intact. Some want a clean exit; others want to stay involved through an earn-out or equity rollover.

Here's the simple secret to success: Having absolute clarity on your goals will guide every decision going forward—from which buyers to approach, to how to structure the deal, to what compromises you're willing to make.

So yes, get clarity. Take as long as it requires, but get clarity.

IDENTIFYING THE IDEAL BUYERS FOR YOU

Not every buyer is good for your business. Your job is to imagine who benefits most from owning your business. Some possibilities:

- Strategic acquirers who gain market reach or capabilities
- Competitors who can fold you in immediately
- Private equity firms that are building a platform in your sector
- Management teams who are looking to buy out the company themselves

Alignment matters. Look for financial capacity, cultural fit, operational synergy, and a vision that works for the people you care about. And here's the veteran's tip: Approach potential buyers quietly. Using trusted advisors through discreet outreach channels is far more effective than blasting your book to everyone with a pulse.

DOING DUE DILIGENCE ALMOST PAINLESSLY

Diligence is where preparation pays off. A buyer will look under every floorboard and behind every firewall they can. Financials, contracts, customer histories, HR files, safety compliance, environmental issues, litigation, tax exposure—all of it will be granularly combed through and catalogued.

Prepared sellers experience diligence like a checklist, not a siege. With organized files, clean EBITDA, diversified revenue streams, and zero skeletons hidden in closets, a due diligence experience can go less like the world's worst proctology exam (though the similarity will still be there!).

The more defensible your business artifacts, the faster diligence moves, the less stress you endure, and the higher your final valuation and exit multiple. It's actually simple math at that point.

TAKING YOUR VALUATION MULTIPLE HIGHER

Multiples are the gravity of M&A. Smaller companies fetch smaller multiples—all other things being equal. But a forward-leaning strategy can change that. That is, as you prepare your business to be acquired, should you also be acquiring complementary businesses yourself, and even running a buildup strategy of your own, integrating these acquisitions onto a common industry-defining platform so that the sum of your enlarged company becomes far greater than the parts? The right acquisitions could even unlock a hypergrowth multiple for you when you do sell it all. That's the ultimate game that a seller can play. But it does require a strong M&A team behind you and access to capital.

STRUCTURING A WIN–WIN–WIN DEAL

A good deal isn't just about money. It's about alignment. Every party—seller, buyer, employees, sometimes even customers—wants to feel that the deal works for them. It can't always, but the more stakeholders the deal satisfies, the greater the likelihood of long-term financial success.

- **Buyers** have one set of priorities based on whether they value stability or flexibility, involvement or hands-off management.
- **Employees** have their own expectations: job security, continued leadership, and cultural continuity.
- **Sellers** have their goals: liquidity, legacy, and personal transition.

A carefully structured deal rewards everyone while keeping incentives aligned long after the ink dries.

NEGOTIATING THE EXIT OF A LIFETIME

Negotiation is often misunderstood. Our minds go to Richard Gere in *Pretty Woman* or Michael Douglas in *Wall Street*. Great dramatic stories. But in the nonfiction world, the best negotiations tend to be the synergistic ones where both sides of the deal feel they've improved their position and can face each other postclose with their respect intact. This is why transparency is critical. Buyers who hide intentions or sellers who gloss over issues create resentment and risk.

Think of it like this: The best deals are conversations, not combat. You're figuring out what everyone truly values, then designing a path where those values are honored. That's how you protect culture, preserve jobs, and secure legacy—without leaving money on the table.

GETTING THROUGH APPROVALS AND THE CLOSING UNSCATHED

The finish line is technical. Regulatory filings, licensing, environmental checks, and legal reviews all converge. Advisors synchronize documents. Funds transfer. Ownership officially changes hands. It's intense—but brief. A well-prepared seller emerges with confidence that the deal reflects the company's true worth.

THINKING AHEAD TO POSTMERGER INTEGRATION

Many sellers make the mistake of treating the sale as an endpoint. It's far from it. Integration begins the moment the wire hits—or ideally before.

- How will your transition occur? Will you remain?
- Will you participate in an earn-out?
- Are you prepared to work as an employee and not an owner?

Clarity here makes the transition smoother, preserves relationships, and reduces surprises down the road.

ASSEMBLING YOUR A-TEAM

Selling a business—whether it's a $10 million family company or a billion-dollar global platform—is a team sport. No single individual can or should carry the deal alone. A successful sale requires a carefully chosen ensemble of specialists whose expertise protects the value you've built up in your business, keeps things moving, and shields you from the kinds of mistakes that can haunt owners long after the deal is done.

Across dozens of transactions, I've learned that bringing in the right people early isn't optional. It is the foundation of the perfect deal.

Investment Bankers

Sit at the center of a professionally run sale process. Their job is simple to outline but remarkably difficult to execute: Create competitive tension and maximize your valuation. A strong banker helps ...

- Shape your story for both strategic and financial buyers.
- Build a curated buyer universe (not simply blast your book to everyone with a pulse).
- Manage outreach, confidentiality, and timelines.
- Control the narrative during management presentations.
- Run the numbers, model different deal structures, and keep pricing pressure high.
- Drive a disciplined, time-bound process that forces buyers to act rather than drift.

When we sold Manitex and H-E Parts, we hired investment banks for exactly these reasons. Early on with H-E Parts, when we were still building our strategic portfolio, we had no such guides. We were the first to attempt a global roll-up strategy in our corner of the mining services industry. It was unmapped terrain, and investment bankers simply didn't know how to advise on something that had never been done.

We were, in every sense, the people "first through the wall."

There's a moment in *Moneyball* that captures the feeling perfectly. Brad Pitt's character, Billy Beane, is told by the Red Sox owner, "The first guy through the wall always gets bloodied. And the people who benefit from the status quo go crazy when you try to change things."

That was us. Bloodied, bruised, and pushing ahead anyway.

But once we had proven the model and built real scale, we absolutely brought in a banker for the exit. And in most sales, bankers are not just helpful—they are indispensable. They create order, competition, and confidence in a process that can easily veer sideways.

The M&A Attorney

Protects your flank. This is not a job for your general counsel or your "Uncle Eddie," who negotiates the building lease each year. M&A law is a specialized craft requiring an attorney who has seen hundreds of deals and knows where danger hides. A great M&A attorney will …

- Uncover hidden liabilities.
- Anticipate the buyer's legal strategies.
- Craft protective representations, warranties, and indemnities.
- Negotiate fine-grain contract terms.
- Structure the deal to avoid postclosing disputes.
- Keep the due diligence process organized and moving.
- Reduce long-term costs by getting the legal work right the first time.

This is the one advisor who may make you mildly uncomfortable, and that's okay. If they seem intimidatingly sharp, that's perfect. Their expertise can shield you from decades of potential fallout—and often saves multiples of their fee by preventing expensive mistakes.

The M&A Accountant

Defends the numbers. A certified public accountant (CPA) who specializes in transactions is worth their weight in gold. They understand the subtleties of deal accounting, purchase-price adjustments, working-capital negotiations, and tax structuring—areas that routinely make or break value. The right M&A accountant will …

- Prepare accurate, defensible financial statements.
- Scrub your EBITDA and normalize add-backs before the buyer does.
- Identify deal-breaking issues early.
- Model tax outcomes across different deal structures.
- Help you navigate rollover equity, earnouts, and seller financing.
- Ensure the quality of earnings report is bulletproof.
- Protect value during the "working capital true-up," where great sums can be lost.

A generalist CPA or small-firm accountant is rarely equipped for this. You want someone who speaks the language of transactions fluently—because the buyer certainly will.

The M&A Advisor

Strategic counselor for the journey. This role can be filled by a seasoned CEO, former owner, or industry expert who has lived through deals from the inside. They help you …

- Prepare the company culturally and operationally for a sale.
- Frame your story in a way that resonates with buyers.
- Understand which buyers are serious and which are tire-kickers.
- Anticipate negotiation dynamics long before they appear.
- Translate banker, lawyer, and accountant jargon into human speak.
- Avoid classic owner mistakes (overpromising, overpricing, waiting too long).

For many sellers—especially first-timers—the advisor becomes the steadying hand. They keep you from making emotional choices, overreacting to buyer demands, or getting distracted by the noise.

Whereas the banker manages the process, and the accountant manages the numbers, the advisor manages you.

BRINGING IT ALL TOGETHER

The perfect deal is never about luck. It's about preparation, alignment, and execution. A strong team, a ready company, and an owner who's evolved with the business produce an outcome that feels almost effortless—because the hard work has been done.

Selling your business is likely the largest financial event of your life. You only get one chance to do it well. Surround yourself with the right people, prepare your company, and approach the process with clarity, courage, and intention. Do that, and you won't just sell a company—you'll secure a legacy.

9 There's No Gap Like a Value Gap

When it comes to unlocking real value in a company, I sometimes feel like Ethel Merman or Frank Sinatra belting out "There's No Business Like Show Business"—big, brassy, unapologetically enthusiastic. Only, instead of footlights and orchestras, my stage is the wide-open space between what a company is and what it could be. If this catchy tune had been about value creation instead, I can hear it going something like this …

There's no gap like a value gap,
It lingers, and it sticks.
Everything about it is revealing,
Yet the market will reward what you fix.
So you'll just go on with that nervous feeling,
Till you close the gap, and now 1 + 1 = 6!

Some business problems can only be solved by getting down on the shop floor, rolling up your sleeves, and figuring out why the dang thing won't run. Other problems are better contemplated at the helm of a Swan 58 somewhere off Santa Monica or out in the blue sweep of Valparaíso Bay, Chile. With a clean breeze wiping any pretense from your face, you gain the kind of clarity that office desks and conference rooms rarely provide. I've found you can hone in on the very heart of how business creates value, which is what it's all about.

As for the heart of business, it comes down to *closing the gaps between strategy and value.* Nowhere have I seen these words better illustrated than with Tadano's January 2025 acquisition of Manitex.

Tadano is Japan's largest manufacturer of cranes and aerial work platforms. Manitex's product line is similar, but at one-tenth the scale and in different markets. Prior to the acquisition, Tadano had watched Manitex for four years and even took a minority stake in the company to see how it would perform with additional investor capital to work with. It was classic Japanese diligence: patient, observant, slow to assume, quick to verify. They wanted to understand not just Manitex's product appeal but its culture, cadences, and commitment to customers.

It was a savvy baby-step approach because, while Manitex had undeniable strengths, the company had been drifting. Revenues had lagged. Scale and margin improvements were not being attained, and a business that was born via acquisition had not coalesced. Manitex had great people and an enviable customer base, but its strategy needed to be refreshed. As a result, the company's stock price had lagged.

Fair to say, Manitex had all the ingredients of a great recipe, but those ingredients were still sitting in the bowl untended.

Being the CEO with the Eye on the Gaps

When I stepped in as CEO two and a half years before the sale that was to come, I knew I had my hands full. This was a classic turnaround situation. The potential was there; the execution was not.

Manitex had spent years acquiring good, solid complementary companies but had then neglected to properly integrate them.

Units in Europe and the US had no incentive to cooperate.

With many different brands operating under one house, customers didn't know what the company stood for.

As for the company's employees, they didn't know what success on the job meant. They were simply not told if they were performing well, poorly, or any other way.

I know I appear to be painting a grim picture, but at the same time, the company had a great line of products, just not tapped. The gap between what Manitex was and what it could be was a couple of soccer fields long. I could not have been more energized for the challenge!

Right out of the gates, we launched the *Elevating Excellence* project. It was a three-year overhaul focused on (a) growing our production capacity by one-third, (b) improving margins by six points, and (c) bringing new discipline to capital allocation. Our financial targets were aggressive: a six-point margin expansion and EBITDA escalating from $6 million to $36 million. These were not blue-sky numbers; they were math married to a plan.

And when we went ahead and hit these marks, suddenly we weren't the problem child in Tadano's eyes anymore. We were a prime strategic asset with—interestingly—an entirely new set of value propositions that could help Tadano close its own value gaps. Just as we'd intended.

THE MAGIC ISN'T IN THE DUE DILIGENCE CHECKLIST

When Tadano began doing serious due diligence on us, readying for a formal offer, we soon dove into the diligence hall of mirrors: inventory counts, IP audits, lease agreements, employment contracts, asset registers, titles, insurance, receivables—the usual checklist.

All necessary.

All important.

All insufficient.

Because none of these things move you from arithmetic to exponential.

No buyer ever tripled the value of a deal because a filing cabinet was organized. The real question, the one that creates real multiples, was this: What strategic value gaps could Tadano close by acquiring Manitex?

WHERE THE MULTIPLIER LIVES

Together, Tadano and Manitex began mapping out the value gaps that we could close in each other.

Market access gaps. Indonesia was a perfect example. Tadano had a strong presence there. Manitex had none. Not because we lacked products, but because we lacked the capital, distribution framework, and local trust to enter the market profitably. Tadano's platform became our runway. One plus one became three.

Product line gaps. Tadano's product family was strong with the biggest equipment buyers, but there were holes at the small-to-mid-sized buyers that Manitex filled beautifully. With Manitex's Italian manufacturing capabilities in tow, Tadano suddenly had offerings they had never been able to present in Asia—and customers there were ready. One plus one became four.

Geographic and political gaps. The 2024 election of Donald Trump reignited "America First" industrial policy. A US-based manufacturing footprint suddenly carried a premium. Manitex didn't just give Tadano a plant—they gained insulation from geopolitical supply chain shocks. One plus one became five.

Operational capability gaps. Our integration plan, margin discipline, product engineering, and revitalized culture gave Tadano a North American engine that was tuned, tested, and accelerating. When you stacked these strategic gaps together, arithmetic went out the window. One plus one became six—the equation went exponential.

THE TRUE WORK OF CLOSING VALUE GAPS

Closing value gaps is not magic. It's not a lucky break or a clever spreadsheet trick. It is strategic diligence, which goes far deeper than financial diligence. Financial diligence tells you what you bought. Strategic diligence tells you what it can become.

This is where sellers, buyers, and their advisors must sit shoulder-to-shoulder, put the P&L aside, and start designing the future. The deal's "multiplier value" emerges only when both sides understand:

- which gaps exist,
- which gaps matter, and
- which gaps can be closed—profitably, reliably, sustainably.

When alignment hits on those three, the fireworks light up the sky.

Valuing a Company Properly

Too many founders and company leaders believe their strategy is self-evident simply because they've lived it. But strategy is only valuable if you can articulate it clearly to someone who has not spent time inside your company.

Selling a business is little different, I suspect, from entering into a marriage. If you don't understand yourself—your habits, blind spots, limitations, goals, values, and quirks—what kind of honest partner can you hope to be?

When a seller can articulate strategy with precision, buyers can instantly see how the business works, how it wins, where its limits are, and how it can enhance the buyer's platform. Without that clarity, buyers default to spreadsheets and shortcuts—reducing your company to commodity metrics and EBITDA discounts.

That is where the classic Three *C*s—Company, Customer, Competition—still do the heavy lifting. If a seller can wrap a clean story around these three *C*s, then the valuation ceiling is going to rise. If not, the conversation sinks into numbers without narrative, and the buyer starts mentally shaving the multiple.

This is why so many buyers begin with the familiar request, "Show me the data." And they're not wrong. Data is the lifeblood of an organization. But today, data is everywhere. Dashboards breed like rabbits after a warm rain. Metrics multiply faster than management capacity.

In this world, Drucker's line—"What gets measured gets managed"—is incomplete. The better question is, "What are the *critical* metrics?" Because collecting more data doesn't guarantee more insight. In fact, it often muddies the water.

A case study of General Electric's Predix platform offers a sobering lesson. Data availability—even mountains of it—does not close value gaps. Predix was born of a kind of Willy Wonka optimism: bold declarations of a new industrial world, promises of near-omniscience, and the belief that if data could be gathered at scale, value would inevitably follow. What followed instead was a costly failure and deeply disappointing returns.

The problem was never a lack of data.

Under Jack Welch and then his successors, GE was already sitting atop some of the richest data environments in the world. Its aviation engines and medical imaging businesses were marvels of instrumentation. Every jet engine in flight was already streaming temperatures, pressures, vibration data, and performance metrics—not just to the cockpit, but to onboard recorders and centralized hubs on the ground. Long before the term AI entered the mainstream, GE could already see almost everything happening inside its most sophisticated machines.

It was tempting—almost inevitable—to believe this capability could be scaled into a new business model: the Industrial Internet of Things (IIoT). GE wasn't alone in this belief. Hitachi, Komatsu, Fluor, and others were drawn into the same vision. The idea was seductive: If you could aggregate and distribute enough data, then insight and, in turn, profit would naturally follow.

That assumption proved false.

Predix ultimately revealed a more uncomfortable truth: The availability of information was not the constraint; the quality of the questions was. GE invested billions in building platforms that could deliver endless data cubes to managers.

In theory, anything could be known. In practice, very little of what was delivered was useful.

Managers were drowning in information without clarity. They were handed oceans of metrics without first being asked questions such as ...

- What are the six data points that actually matter?
- At what cadence—every five minutes, daily, weekly—do they create insight?
- What decisions do they inform?
- What outcomes do customers actually care about?

Without disciplined inquiry, data becomes noise. Worse, it becomes paralyzing. Organizations slip into the belief that data itself is magic—that if they simply mine enough of it, meaning will emerge. Instead, they find themselves mired in a kind of analytical sludge: endless dashboards, endless reports, and no clearer understanding of what to do next.

Data is a blessing. A preponderance of data, without purpose, is a curse.

The power of data is unlocked not by accumulation, but by intention. It begins with asking the right questions—questions anchored in customer value, operational reality, and decision-making relevance. Only then does timeliness matter. Only then do metrics sharpen rather than blur judgment.

Predix didn't fail because GE lacked information. It failed because the organization mistook access for insight. And that distinction—between knowing everything and knowing what matters—is where real value is either created or destroyed.

So before a company builds a dashboard or hands a scorecard to an employee to keep track of work product, it should ask questions such as:

- What truly moves our business?

- What data helps us serve customers better?
- What data helps our employees win?
- What data helps our investors see our forward trajectory?

An aviation shop is going to need real-time telemetry. A machine shop probably doesn't. A distribution company might obsess over on-time delivery. A software firm might obsess over churn. Context matters. And the right question is always, "Why does this metric matter, and to whom?"

When a company focuses on the right metrics, it gains the insight needed to value itself properly. And only then can the real work begin: identifying and closing the value gaps that transform a good company into a great investment.

Closing the Value Gaps

So what actually closes a value gap? Three areas can be focused on.

1. TALENT—THE ULTIMATE MULTIPLIER

Nothing amplifies potential value capture faster than a strengthened bench. Buyers need to see a company of stellar performers. Not just one or two, but across the board. With a leadership team that thinks strategically, a finance function that is disciplined and anticipatory, engineers and operators who understand the product deeply, and managers who can scale the business without compromising the culture that has made it great.

Financial buyers, in particular, see talent as the safest predictor of future performance. They know that if the people are strong, the numbers are likely to follow. This fully suggests that personnel changes may be in order in the lead-up to an M&A event.

2. MARGINS—LEVERS THAT CAN BE PULLED

Few companies can boast perfect profit margins, and buyers don't expect them to. What they do expect is evidence that the levers are being worked. This means turning intention into action.

- **Strengthen pricing authority** with initiatives such as tightening discount discipline, raising prices where value supports it, and training the sales team to sell on outcomes, not concessions.
- **Shift toward a diversified product mix** that emphasizes higher-margin SKUs and adjacent offerings that may lift blended profitability.
- **Drive supply-chain efficiencies** through vendor consolidation, smarter procurement, longer-term contracts, and better demand forecasting to reduce waste and volatility.
- **Improve labor productivity** with clearer workflows, better tooling and automation, cross-training, and aligning incentives for improvements in key metrics such as throughput, quality, and uptime.
- **Unlock product upgrade opportunities** by refreshing legacy lines, introducing premium tiers, and adding features that customers will gladly pay more for.
- **Leverage SG&A** by eliminating duplicative processes, optimizing systems, and scaling shared services so that overhead grows more slowly than revenue.
- **Increase channel efficiency** by focusing on the highest-ROI distributors, eliminating underperforming partners, and directing sales efforts where margin impact is highest.

A company that understands these levers—and can show how future margin growth will come from actively working them—

commands a stronger multiple. Margins don't need to be perfect. They simply need to be credibly improving.

3. PROCESSES—THE WAY A BUSINESS SCALES

Everyday business processes are proofs of value. They show buyers how new customers will be found, how work will be delivered, how quality will be ensured, how employees will be nurtured within a nested company culture, and how performance will be measured.

When you think about it, what buyers really want to know is, "Can this business scale without breaking?" These everyday business process tools (scorecards, routines, checklists, operating cadences) matter because they first reduce the risks of the deal in the buyer's eyes, then they can accelerate the integration process, and lastly, they can ensure that the business doesn't melt down upon transfer.

When a seller can document these everyday processes—not just speak about how we do things around here, but carefully document them—the perceived risk of acquisition plummets and the multiple that will be paid for the business rises.

The Buyer's Thesis

Whether aware of it or not, every buyer puts together a thesis—a reason for going ahead with a high-risk, high-stakes deal when there are so many unknowns and so much can go wrong. Having a thesis is essential if longevity is the objective. Whether an acquirer in the wild world of M&A is a cowboy or a bean counter—and there are plenty of both—the deal has to pan out, or a lot of money is going down the drain.

For this reason, the buyer's thesis begins and ends with EBITDA projections, but along the way, a number of questions have to be satisfactorily answered. Buyers—especially strategic buyers—have to satisfactorily answer these top ten critical questions:

1. How does this business add value to our ongoing operations?
2. What new markets does it unlock that we cannot reach today?
3. Do we gain geographic advantages we don't currently have?
4. What manufacturing, engineering, or product capabilities strengthen our position?
5. Will this business's team be a good fit with our existing team?
6. Does the business's product line cross-pollinate with our existing portfolio?
7. Does the acquisition improve our finances, stock price, and investor expectations?
8. Will we encounter any intractable regulatory or cultural roadblocks?
9. Does this deal multiply value—not just add to it?
10. Most importantly, how confident are we in reaching that goal line?

The stronger the buyer's thesis, the higher the valuation—pure and simple. So a seller wants to make sure these questions are all answerable. That's actually the easier part of the M&A dance.

What happens from the seller's perspective when no such buyer's thesis appears to be operative?

It does sometimes happen that a buyer has the resources to buy and just wants to buy. It also happens that buyers have only a vague thesis in mind, and if pressed, would have to admit to being unclear on the purpose of the deal. In these cases, buyers are like sailors without a compass—they may move, but not necessarily in a meaningful direction.

In these cases, if the seller is still motivated to see the deal go forward and not sideways, the seller may have to take the lead in charting the path forward. Here, it helps for the seller to recognize the signs of a weak thesis and be prepared to meet the buyer halfway—to keep things on track.

Seller Crib Sheet for Attacking Weak Buyer Thesis

- **If lack of strategic rationale.** Buyer can't explain why the acquisition fits or what they plan to do with it. So you bring them back to first principles. Ask them to articulate the future state they're trying to build—markets, capabilities, customers—and then help them connect the dots.
- **If no postmerger integration plan.** Buyer assumes the post-merger integration will be "plug and play," which it never is. So gently but firmly outline what integration really requires. Offer a high-level integration road map—systems, people, customers—and figure out how it will be resourced.
- **If inadequate cultural due diligence.** Poor cultural alignment kills more deals than numbers ever will. So open the hood for them. Describe how your people think, work, communicate, and make decisions. Show how your culture can align with their culture. Nobody can expect cultures to align overnight, only that it's very likely to happen over time.
- **If assuming the business will just keep working.** Ignoring key processes and systems, talent dependencies, and customer relationships is a recipe for failure. So you should walk them through the invisible machinery: your most critical people's

deep talents, the tribal knowledge you've accumulated, the customer touchpoints that you've built up. Explain what breaks if they mishandle this machinery; buyers need to grasp the fragility before they can steward the value.

- **If underestimating the complexities.** If a buyer says, "This should be simple," you know you've fallen into the land of wishful thinking. You want this deal to succeed, so you should surface all of the complexities of the deal with none of the dramatics. Show the interdependencies, the bottlenecks, the regulatory or operational quirks. Complexity isn't bad if laid out on the table, but it can kill a deal if swept under the table.
- **If ignoring customer and vendor implications.** Every M&A deal steadily ripples outward, and buyers must be able to manage the unknowable effects that outlie. So ask the buyer how they plan to communicate with customers and vendors, and when. If there's no plan, help them sketch one. Deals can go sideways when stakeholders feel blindsided.
- **If chasing trends instead of strategy.** Acquiring for optics or the latest business fad can result in a lousy outcome. So inquire about the buyer's long-term value creation thinking. Ask how the acquisition strengthens their core capabilities or strategic direction. If they can't anchor the deal to strategy, it's not a deal—it's a distraction. You may be okay with that! But be clear on what you're seeing because …

A weak buyer's thesis almost always leads to postclose disappointment of some sort, usually including downward pressure on valuation. And that can blow back on the seller—even if the seller parts ways with the acquirer after the deal. So the seller's job is to surface the gaps early, guide the buyer toward clarity, and protect the value built up. When both sides align on a credible thesis, the deal becomes safer, smoother, more lucrative.

Though we've only just touched on the basics of valuation here, it should be clear that the point of "gap closing" is not about detailed spreadsheets or compelling pitch decks. It's about understanding strategy, articulating it clearly, and aligning it with a buyer's ability to multiply value.

When both sides see the same future and can describe it in concrete terms, the gap closes, the value rises, and the deal becomes more than a transaction. It becomes as powerful as Ethel Merman or Frank Sinatra belting out "There's No Gap Like a Value Gap!" And there's no more rewarding moment in business than watching two companies close that gap together—turning one plus one into six.

A Nested Culture—The Ultimate Hat Trick

Shortly after joining Manitex as CEO, I set out to meet with our top customers and investors, and as many employees as possible. I recall the sentiments of one long-standing investor who stated, "We are long in the stock and would characterize Manitex's performance as 'surviving.' What we want for the business is for it to 'thrive.'" This statement resonated with me for months, and I found the same desire for the business from our customers and key employees. Our customers, investors, and employees all wanted to see the business succeed. They wanted Manitex to thrive.

Despite the criticisms, I was encouraged. I was not expecting such goodwill from key stakeholders. Manitex's line of heavy machinery (booms, cranes, aerial lifts) was impressive by many measures. But this asset base was not being optimized. The market knew this—Manitex's stock had been underperforming for years.

Its customers knew this—they liked the various brands of equipment they could buy or rent from Manitex, but brand association was low, and that tamped down sales.

Its employees knew this—they would go months and even years without any feedback from management on whether they were performing well or not.

Its board knew this too—that's why I was hired.

In years prior, Manitex had gone out and gobbled up fourteen brands to add to its existing manufacturing business. Each acquisition was a good one, names that were known in the space: Badger Equipment, Load King Trailers, CVS Ferrari, Schaeff Forklifts, PM Group, Oil & Steel, Valla, Sabre Manufacturing, LiftKing, Crane & Machinery.

Manitex's acquisition strategy had been deliberately broad, since it aimed to build an industry-defining platform encompassing cranes, forklifts, hauling systems, container handling, and support. This diversified footprint was meant to take the company beyond the crane OEM it began as, into different sectors: rough-terrain cranes, boom trucks, container handling/reach-stackers, forklifts for indoor and rough terrain, hauling/trailer systems, specialized tanks, and crane distribution/service operations.

Yes, a lot. And on paper, it was a brilliant buildup idea—putting together a broad lifting plus handling plus infrastructure platform.

Such breadth of complexity could also give Manitex optionality. When markets shifted as they perennially did (e.g., construction is down, but container handling is up), different brands on the platform could cushion the company through the cycles.

This breadth of complexity could only work, however, if all the acquired brands were effectively integrated under the Manitex banner and, more importantly, if the acquired companies could coalesce around a common global aim.

But that hadn't happened. The company had only four viable product lines, but it had thirteen brands in-house. And those brands weren't getting along too well. Teams in Europe were disconnected from teams in the US, leaving customers constantly confused about who was on first and what was on second. This corporate Abbott & Costello act only got worse when, upon closer inspection, it was clear that several of the brands made so little sense to the customers that they should have been decommissioned years back.

In my first presentation to the board, I outlined a plan. It was April, and there were nine months remaining in the fiscal year. I would (a) evaluate and diagnose the company for three months, (b) test a series of hypotheses and develop a strategic plan for three months, then (c) submit the plan and budget for the following fiscal year. The board was ready to review and approve a new strategy for the company by December of that year. It would be a three-year plan, later called *Elevating Excellence*. Internally, the employees and I called it our path to becoming a thriving business.

My aim would be to put the **G.A.L.E. Force** to work identifying and communicating Manitex's global aim, while empowering local teams to execute on this strategy within their markets.

Job number one was to diagnose Manitex's problems and develop a solution to improve our EBITDA performance. If we could get that balance right, I believed something powerful could happen. Local teams could feel seen, trusted, and energized. Customers could recognize that Manitex understood their markets—not from a distance, but within the rhythm of their daily realities. Rather than constraining performance, we could begin to amplify it.

Done well, this approach could do more than improve operations or margins. It could reshape the company's identity. Manitex could become globally coherent and locally vibrant—an uncommon combination in heavy industry. And in achieving that, we would substantiate the right to make further investments.

If it worked, it would be the ultimate hat trick: a unified global strategy, a highly engaged team, and a business that measured success on the upswing. We would then have the right to expand through M&A.

In short, we would first fix the performance of Manitex and then position it to grow through M&A.

What I didn't know at the time was which strategic player in the heavy equipment industry would ultimately come knocking. Not sure I could've predicted that Tadano—a $2.3 billion Japanese global crane manufacturer—would be the buyer for the $223 million Manitex after we spent thirty months reshaping the business. But I did know this: If we executed on the blueprint with precision, Manitex would be healthier and have a mandate to grow through acquisition or be attractive for acquisition. Quality attracts quality. It always has.

Those thirty months taught me more about change, culture, and value creation than any textbook ever could. What follows is my attempt to distill that experience into a **G.A.L.E. Force** framework that any company could use to guide its own market ambitions.

Building a Nested Culture Within Legacy Canyons

I like to think of culture the way a geologist thinks of water. A slow-moving stream may not look powerful, but give it enough time, and it will carve its way through mountain rock. A company's culture does the same thing with its structures and processes. Over time, its preferences, biases, and rituals carve grooves into the organization. Work flows through those grooves. Decisions travel through those grooves. Communication, trust, conflict, creativity—everything slides into the paths that culture has worn.

This permanence is why tiny attempts at change get washed away. Try one new workflow? The old habits swallow it. Launch a light "values refresh"? The canyon walls don't even echo back. Announce a new customer promise without changing incentives or behaviors? The cultural current sweeps it right downstream.

The good news is that carving new channels is entirely possible. It just requires the right kind of disruption. You have to push in the right way, with a single magnitude greater than the culture's current force, before the river bends in a new direction. So yes, culture can change, but rarely politely.

Coordinated cultural change requires doing several things at once in a cross-reinforcing way so the organization experiences a coherent shift instead of feeling subjected to a series of uncomfortable nudges. To nest a culture within a business of multiple local cultures or histories, here are some helpful steps.

DEFINE THE NONNEGOTIABLES

The first step is to define your global identity. We discussed this already, but it cannot be overstated. When I arrived, Manitex had a two-decade history of acquiring and selling various businesses. The age of the business units acquired ranged from twenty-four years to eighty years, and they had differing ownership structures. Most of the acquired businesses were spun off from another corporation, a corporate carve-out. In addition to their brand history, these businesses were located in four US states: Italy, Romania, Chile, and Argentina.

That first visit to our operations in Northern Italy was telling. On my last day there, to make a point, I asked the local management team a question. "During this week, you have been generous to teach me what you do, to help me understand your history and challenges, and introduce me to your teams. Thank you. My question is, who are we?"

Truly, the business had an identity crisis.

To build a cohesive strategy, we needed to have a cohesive identity, a Manitex culture. It could not be an offense to the business's legacy. It had to complement the strategy, and it had to serve each of the business units. This is where the core values came in. It allowed us to identify a short list of fundamental principles that, all taken together, would define who we are locally and how we support our global ambition.

SEPARATE IDENTITY FROM PRACTICE

Identity defines who we are globally and what must be true everywhere. Practices define how it becomes true everywhere. Many cultures clash because companies confuse who we are with how we work. Many American companies struggle with European holiday schedules. The month of August, in Europe, can be very frustrating for an American company. The fallacy is to believe that productivity is always better when we work longer. This is not always the case. In fact, our Italian operations were quicker and more adept at meeting our production target improvements than our US-based team.

Identity must be informed by global purpose, common values, and standards. There is risk, however, in equating local practice with identity. Our US-based factory would begin production daily at 6:00 a.m., while our Chilean and Italian teams would begin at 8:00 a.m. Was one practice better than another? Of course not.

It is important to allow for local norms to continue while building a nested culture. This would include meeting cadence, communication styles, localized decision processes, and vendor relationships.

When building a nested culture, resist the temptation to equate practice with identity.

EMBRACE CULTURAL TRANSLATION; RESIST CULTURAL IMPOSITION

When we surveyed key employees to decide on Manitex's core values, in the US, there were references to perseverance and dedication. In Italy and Argentina, the adjective was passion. In reality, those surveyed were talking about the same principle. They were expressing their commitment and dedication to the business.

It is helpful to build a culture within a culture through translation. For example, instead of reinforcing customer service as a principle, one might ask open-ended questions such as:

- "What does customer obsession look like here?"
- "How and when do our employees feel a sense of ownership with the company?"
- "Can you tell me a story of unsurpassed dedication this past year?"

It's also good to avoid forcing terminology on a team before understanding the local cultural clues. Declaring, "This is how we do things now!" or even "Our new core values state this, therefore we must …" will miss two great opportunities:

- **Learning.** Using translation to understand and communicate core values will allow you, as a leader, a front-row seat to learn what works locally.
- **Empowerment.** Using translation will also enable your team to devise a localized approach or set of executables. And believe me, the local team knows how to do it better than the new kid on the block or the corporate team flying in for a quarterly business review.

M&A used to mean one thing: assimilation. The acquired unit was expected to bend, conform, and adopt the parent company's systems, norms, and cadence. In today's multicultural era, M&A is less about assimilation and more about translation.

Translation is not passive. It is active. It is the art of meaning-making. It asks, "How can our global systems express themselves authentically in the local language and rhythm?"

Postmerger integration is best facilitated by translators. They craft multilingual organizations that honor the strengths of local operators while equipping them with globally efficient systems. This is **G.A.L.E. Force** in action. Success is measured not only in financial synergies, but in cultural fluency—the invisible engine that turns potential into performance.

ANCHOR CORE VALUES IN LEADERSHIP

Good people attract good people. This is a universal principle. If a team is well-led and marked by engaged and unified team members, that team will naturally attract others who share the same values.

Your core values, the identity of your nested culture, should be the anchor for every new hire, promotion, and leader development program. After identifying the Manitex identity and core values, we quickly moved to change our people processes.

- We added our core values to every performance appraisal.
- We added core value questions and themes to our hiring processes.
- We instituted the Elevating Excellence Core Value Awards.

When developing our leadership, we would seek out individuals who naturally lived out our core values. These actions were vital to demonstrating our resolve and our commitment to these core values.

LEVERAGE CROSS-DIVISION RESPONSIBILITIES

Shortly after HCM acquired H-E Parts, they asked us for a list of high-potential leaders within the company. Some of these were presented with an opportunity to take an assignment in Tokyo, at HCM's headquarters. This cross-cultural experience is not something that all companies can do. It is expensive and time-consuming. The principle that HCM was following, however, is a brilliant one. They were seeking to know and be known to the company they had just acquired.

Cross-company or cross-cultural experiences can be attained economically. With Manitex, we did this in the following effective ways:

- **Performance bonuses.** We tied senior leadership bonuses, in part, to the performance of their peers.
- **Project teams.** Critical projects, associated with *Elevating Excellence,* were given to teams within different business units. These teams were charged with project oversight; their regular

work together helped build a corporate identity and reinforce our core values.

- **Quarterly business reviews.** Often, we asked for division leaders and/or managers to attend quarterly business reviews and travel internationally to participate in the business reviews of other divisions.
- **Tradeshows.** On one occasion, we asked the factory floor to nominate two peers to attend the largest tradeshow in our industry, CONEXPO. The nominations were designed to identify team members who exemplified our core values. There was a catch, however. The nominees were charged with an assignment at the tradeshow and would need to give a report to the whole factory upon their return. One of our quality technicians, Ray Ramirez, attended in 2023, and the presentation he gave upon his return was legendary. Ray has since been promoted to product specialist with Tadano Manitex.

REINFORCE YOUR CULTURE WITH STORIES

Engaged employees are employees who know their company and are known by their company. Regardless of where you are in the world, people appreciate being recognized. As long as the story is authentic and sincere, it will be appreciated by your team. As CEO, you are the "communicator in chief" and have charge of communication of your strategy.

G.A.L.E. Force requires a coherent and clearly communicated strategy. This is the job of senior leadership. Your business culture, the culture you are developing as a result of M&A, will need regular reinforcements. Relaying the successes of your team and TGR stories (Things Going Right) will aid you along these lines.

Remember, the *E* in DRiiVE is a strong "team-based" ego. By telling the right stories, you can reward your people for a job well done, reinforce your identity and core values, and build a culture that transcends time zones, history, and geography. It has never been easier to do this in this age of social media. At Manitex, we used the following:

- **Newsletters.** Our quarterly newsletter, named *Elevate*, was initially written by me, as the new CEO. However, we added other members of the executive committee to take on sections every quarter. By design, we would highlight one or two core values in every issue. *Elevate* was published in English, Italian, Spanish, Romanian, and French. These issues were broadly distributed and found in every breakroom.
- **Videos.** We held our first annual strategy meeting in August 2022. This was a first for Manitex, and it was used to help me and the executive committee define our global strategy (the GA or Global Ambition in **G.A.L.E. Force**). The work was meaningful and memorable and became the basis of *Elevating Excellence*, released January 2023. We created a video to introduce the strategy to all team members. This was followed by local sessions with division leadership to outline the strategy and then lead discussions regarding local executables and calls to action.
- **LinkedIn and social media.** We leveraged our social-media platforms to promote our product, our customers, and our people. We would season these posts with our core values, again with an aim to promote and reinforce them.

HOW CUSTOMERS EXPERIENCE YOUR CULTURE

It can be easy for company leaders to forget that customers often already know your culture. Sometimes they know it better than you do—because they're looking into the fishbowl with their interests in mind, whereas you're in the fishbowl.

Customers feel it in every email, every call, every service interaction, every delay, every uninformed surprise. You can't hide culture from them. If your internal culture is energized, curious, attentive, and hungry to serve, customers feel it immediately. If your culture is sluggish, siloed, defensive, or apathetic, they feel that even faster.

Ask people about their favorite companies, as I often do on my morning walks, and their responses are revealing. People don't use words like "Company A has aligned internal values," of course. But they do talk about how a company made them feel or how they get treated like someone who matters. That is culture, writ large.

This is why regularly surveying customers, and doing it properly, is the fastest and often most accurate diagnostic of your company's operations.

WHEN A CULTURAL PROBLEM IS HIDING

Some cultural issues hide below the waterline; it happens most often when the issue involves the senior management team. This team can look healthy from the outside and still be quietly eroding the corporate foundations.

A few of the most dangerous patterns include:

- **Happy talk.** Leaders avoid hard truths, congratulate themselves too easily, and make lists of things to "look into" when they find the time. This is common with profitable, high-gross-margin businesses. Everything is funny when you are making money. Less so when faced with a bank covenant or negative investor sentiment.

- **Complacency.** Goals are set low enough that success is guaranteed—and the bar gradually sinks.
- **Silos.** Leaders protect turf instead of building bridges; collaboration becomes optional because "my lane" is the only thing that matters.

These problems are subtle because they masquerade as harmony. But they can erode performance. As the saying goes, a fish rots from the head. The personalities of the executive team leave a signature on the company. Their habits become assumptions. Their beliefs become norms. Their blind spots become landmines others have to tiptoe around.

Culture starts at the top—always.

A CEO's job doesn't begin at the office on Monday morning. Being CEO is a lifestyle career. Your conduct, words, and actions are on display 24-7. Your behavior in town or at a public event is on display. Just ask Andy Byron and Kristin Cabot, formerly of Astronomer. These two are better known as the "Kiss Cam" couple. It may not be fair, but it is true.

So to own leadership, be certain to …

- **Be authentic.** Be yourself and make certain you can support and live by core values.
- **Be overt.** Look for opportunities to reinforce and highlight the core values.
- **Be overcommunicative.** Teams crave feedback, so be present to listen.
- **Value transparency.** For it is closely allied with trust, which is always Job #1.

11

Aligning Cultures Before and After the Close

When Company A sets out to acquire or merge with Company B, the due diligence machine roars to life. There's a checklist as long as your arm—financials to reconcile, contracts to inventory, assets to verify, risks to price. It's thorough. It's disciplined. And almost always, one item on that list gets treated like a footnote: culture.

For many M&A professionals, culture is handled like seasoning—something you sprinkle on the soup after it's already cooked. But culture isn't the seasoning; it's in the broth. And if you don't understand what's in that broth before you sit down for the meal—or before you buy the restaurant, since we're applying this idea to M&A—it's already too late to fix the flavor.

Understanding the culture of a business to be acquired can be difficult to ascertain. Deal diligence is typically limited to senior managers and selected professionals. Talking to them won't reveal much about what's in the company soup, or how the business really operates. For a variety of reasons, the required access to the workforce and middle management simply won't make itself available until after the deal is closed.

Pre-merger cultural diligence should remain on the table and a formal part of the process. The real **G.A.L.E. Force** work begins the day after the closing table, but you can and should start building your knowledge base. Doing so forces you to understand which elements of a target's value are inseparable from its local environment, which cultural traits are sacred and must be protected, and which habits or norms may quietly poison execution after the deal closes. Just as importantly, it helps answer the most basic question of all: Should this deal happen at all?

Strategy can sparkle. Operations can shine. Financial models can be engineered to impress. It will be the postclose execution and postmerger cultural integration, however, that make or break the deal long-term. As we have discussed, culture is where deals ultimately live or die. It determines how decisions get made, how conflict gets resolved, how trust is earned, and how quickly momentum builds or stalls once the ink is dry.

That is why pre-merger cultural diligence isn't a soft exercise, but hard work.

Map the Cultures Before You Sign

We've likened culture to a broth, but technically it's best to think of it as an operating system. Two systems can't run side by side—or merge—without understanding how each one is built. Culture mapping gives you that blueprint. It asks questions such as:

- How do people communicate?
- How are decisions made?
- Can a decision tree be identified?
- Who holds influence behind the scenes?
- Who stays or leaves voluntarily?
- Who should be rewarded and for what reasons?
- How does the business anticipate and deal with conflict?

Create a Cultural Map:

The organizational equivalent of a topographical chart showing peaks (strengths), valleys (weak spots), cliffs (danger zones), and bridges (points of alignment). The map should identify …

- Decision-making structures
- Communication norms
- Feedback style
- Leadership expectations
- Attitudes toward accountability
- Work pace and scheduling
- Conflict style
- Employee empowerment levels
- Symbols, rituals, and unwritten rules

This map tells you not just where you align, but how hard the integration is going to be and where you'll need your "A-Team."

Skip these questions, and you're inviting integration headaches. Good deals can turn into painful integrations, and painful integrations into value write-downs.

It is best to find opportunities for informal discussions, opportunities where a safe discussion can happen. This is easier to accomplish with smaller companies. In the past, I have gone on hikes, asked for a tour of their hometown during visits, or taken in a sporting event together. Many of my acquisitions were of founder-led businesses. I make it a practice to invite them and their partners for dinner. The process is helpful to both parties, who can learn about the acquired and acquiring businesses. The larger the deal, the more formal the process. The point is, make it a priority to understand as much about their culture as you can.

In some cases, you may be able to outsource or produce a cultural audit. This is rare, and in reality, only a very small portion of M&A deals perform this and/or allow for it. The larger and more structured the deal, the more difficult it will be to map the target company's culture. Regardless, you should be producing a map or a system of how things get done.

This map is not some HR survey or a series of polite chats with executives. Indeed, I've found that the leaders of a company often have the rosiest—and least accurate—view of its own culture. To see the real picture, you need data from the whole organism. You are looking to pick up …

- Values people actually practice (not the ones on the lobby wall)
- How information moves (slowly? urgently? sideways?)
- How conflict shows up (open debate? quiet avoidance?)
- How decisions are made (by consensus? charisma? command?)
- Hidden friction patterns (e.g., engineering versus sales, headquarters versus the field, legacy employees versus new hires)

Cultural diligence often misses subtle social signals that can derail integration: local labor norms, environmental expectations, gender equity, definitions of fairness. Regulatory approval isn't the same as cultural license—you need both.

For cross-border or regionally entrenched deals, local cultural stakeholder mapping is every bit as critical as the internal company mapping you are doing. Be sure to clearly identify and understand the reach and potential impact of

- regulation and regulating authorities,
- community leaders,
- labor groups,
- suppliers, and
- cultural institutions.

Evaluate their power, priorities, alliances, and likely reactions. Done well, this step can shorten approvals or prevent a culturally disastrous acquisition.

Identify Cultural Deal Makers and Breakers

Every deal has people who bridge worlds—managers fluent in both local and corporate language, equally at home on the plant floor or in the boardroom. These individuals are priceless. Pre-merger diligence should locate them, retain them, and celebrate them. They can be the shock absorbers when two cultures first begin bumping into each other.

Every deal also has nonnegotiables. In finance, it's valuation. In operations, it's customer retention. On the cultural front, the non-negotiables are often hidden in subtler behaviors. Some cultures just don't blend. A consensus-driven organization can't instantly behave like an agile start-up. If integration requires rewiring a company's entire nervous system, you need to know before signing.

Lenses for a Cultural Audit

- **Quantitative surveys:** Anonymous, company-wide, focused on behaviors, not slogans.
- **Employee focus groups:** Randomly selected participants, not handpicked top performers.
- **One-on-one interviews:** Across hierarchy, geography, and tenure. Frontline employees often reveal what leadership has forgotten—or never knew.

Hone In on the Cultural Value Proposition

Every company has those things that make it succeed. Some are quite tangible: distribution networks, proprietary technology. Others are cultural: brand heritage, community trust, tacit know-how, and informal networks. In doing diligence, the goal is very clearly to (a) spot those assets that are inextricably linked to the current culture and (b) figure out what happens if they are disrupted. Breaking the wrong part can erase the value you just paid for.

Most often, there are five cultural icons or strengths that you break at possibly terminal risk:

- A beloved brand deeply rooted in local identity
- A distribution network maintained through long-standing personal relationships
- Tacit know-how that only lives in experienced employees' heads

- Community trust earned over decades
- Informal networks, alliances, or rituals that outsiders never see

Cultural Behaviors That Are Difficult to Reconcile

- **Time orientation:** Consensus-driven versus fast, top-down
- **Risk tolerance:** Careful planners versus bold experimenters
- **Power distribution:** Egalitarian versus hierarchical
- **Trust formation:** Relationship-based versus task-based
- **Communication style:** Subtle versus blunt

Align Leadership Early (Very Early)

Before the merger agreement is signed, leaders must talk—not just about all the synergies they hope to be creating (the usual stuff) but also about how they lead their troops (harder to define; equally important).

Executives often have deeply ingrained styles. Some rely on consensus; others move fast and expect the organization to keep up. Some are transparent; others operate on a need-to-know basis. Some love structure; others run on improvisation and hustle.

If two companies are coming together, and especially if the acquired CEO is packaged up in the deal, the two CEOs' styles matter. If these styles are wildly incompatible, the cultural cost of merging the organizations could easily outweigh the strategic benefit of the deal itself. I've seen CEOs agree on strategy in twenty minutes but disagree on decision-making for twenty months. Better to know that up front.

Standardize Versus Localize

Should Usually Standardize

- Compliance
- Financial controls
- Data governance
- Cybersecurity
- Executive reporting
- Core HR policies

Should Usually Localize

- Marketing
- Product design
- Customer experience
- Local partnerships
- Community-facing roles

Decide Which Is Global, Which Is Local

The whole idea behind the **G.A.L.E. Force** framework is that parts of the company benefit from global standardization, and other parts benefit from a localized execution. So strategic choices must be made about which processes, policies, and systems need a consistent, global approach, and which are best left flexible to honor local realities.

Some functions demand consistency because they form the backbone of corporate governance, protect the enterprise, or ensure compliance with global standards. Skimp here, and you risk regulatory breaches, cybersecurity snafus, or financial misstatements that can undo even the best strategic deal.

Other functions, however, thrive on localization. Marketing campaigns, product design, customer engagement, and community-facing initiatives often rely on deep knowledge of local culture, preferences, and expectations. Standardizing these too aggressively can dilute brand resonance, alienate customers, and erode the very value that made an acquisition target attractive.

The art of pre-merger diligence is knowing where to draw the line—protecting the global spine while nurturing local lifeblood. Done right, this allows the merged entity to capture scale and efficiency without sacrificing the unique capabilities that drive success on the ground.

Define Local Measures of Success

The bottom line is this: Pre-merger cultural diligence isn't a luxury, and it certainly isn't a soft skill. It is the work. When you understand the culture you're buying into—and when you respect and preserve the local magic—you build a stronger, more resilient enterprise. You start turning cultural markers into financial equivalents. Suddenly, culture isn't an intangible you gesture toward; it's a measurable multiplier of value.

Blowing Away Barriers to Cultural Alignment

Talented men and women are drawn to M&A. It represents a challenge and way to exponentially expand both the size and value of the enterprise. And the best of them know the game isn't won through financial engineering or brilliant strategic maneuvering alone. It's won on the far less tidy terrain of culture, which is, at its core, applied psychology. Deals rise and fall on the quirks, instincts, insecurities, and aspirations of ordinary people doing extraordinary things.

From the person running the forklift to the person running the boardroom, we are emotional creatures—steady one day, volatile the next, but always trying to bring our best to the table. And it's inside this messy, marvelous human tangle that M&A either unlocks value or loudly destroys it.

Over time, I've learned that four of these messy human behaviors consistently wiggle their way into every deal. They can obscure or illuminate goals, distort or clarify communication, block or break open insights. When written down on paper, these behaviors look plenty obvious. In the heat of a transaction, they are anything but.

The four are: how people communicate, how they use language, how they relate to hierarchy, and how they make decisions.

Recognizing these four factors as either impediments or enablers is half the battle. The other half is facing them directly—much like a sailor tacking into a headwind. You don't wish the wind away; you work with its force, pivot deliberately, and use its resistance to carry you forward.

COMMUNICATION IS ALWAYS THE FIRST BARRIER

Some cultures operate in a high-context mode—where meaning lives between the lines, in shared histories, subtleties, and relationships. Others run on low context—direct, explicit, and comfortable with blunt clarity. Either approach can work just fine, so long as everyone knows the rules of the room and feels safe operating within them.

I think of a US manager who spotted a flaw in an equipment design while visiting a Japanese field office. She did what any competent American manager would do: She documented the problem in an email, copied her boss, copied the Japanese team, and laid out the issues plainly. Her boss appreciated the straight talk. Her Japanese colleagues were mortified. She had violated a deeply held norm: Problems should be raised privately, gently, and in a way that preserves harmony.

Had the US woman simply posed her concern as a question—"What might happen if this widget doesn't perform as expected?"—her Japanese teammates would have investigated, reached the same conclusion, and preserved the relationship. A simple, nuanced change in email sentence structures would have changed the entire arc of the interaction.

Western cultures tend to be low context; we are generally comfortable with straightforward questions. "Do you prefer option A or option B?" is a question we can handle. In high-context cultures, however, this same question can feel blunt or even confrontational.

Context takes on added importance when it escalates from field reports to negotiations, for instance. Here, the players must be adept at inferring a counterpart's interest in priorities from subtle shifts in tone, or in a hesitation, or what is left unsaid. Reading these cues correctly is how barriers are lowered, decisions are expedited, tensions are abated, and critical information is surfaced for action steps to be taken.

LANGUAGE AND FLUENCY ARE LESSER BARRIERS

English may be the international language of business, but fluency isn't evenly distributed—and accents, idioms, and speed of speech can create hidden fractures in collaboration.

On my early-morning walks during Latin American visits, I've had countless conversations about this. A Peruvian oil-and-gas consultant once told me, "I have very good questions, but I cannot always express them. The American member speaks fast and leads everything. I feel like my ideas stay in my head."

Another morning, a Mexican engineer put it this way, "In my culture, humility matters. Even if you know the answer, you pose it as a question. Americans think that means I'm unsure or inexperienced. They don't realize I am being respectful."

Both men were sharp, capable, and carrying mission-critical knowledge. But cultural and linguistic differences meant their contributions weren't being fully heard or valued. When local experts like them aren't able to contribute freely, projects tend to falter.

HIERARCHY AND AUTHORITY ARE THE TRICKY BARRIERS

A business fashion since the late 1990s has been to configure teams in deliberately flat structures to spark collaboration and speed. It works well—until those same teams must collaborate with partners who operate inside deeply hierarchical organizations. A flat-model employee expects parity and quick decisions; a hierarchical employee respects the chain of command and escalates each step. The collision can be jarring.

During one Korean–US negotiation held on American soil, these differences became painfully clear. Each time the US team requested information, their Korean counterparts dutifully escalated questions up the ladder. The Americans read the pauses as obstruction and grew increasingly frustrated by the stop-and-go rhythm. The Korean team, mortified by the Americans' visible irritation, offered small concessions simply to keep the discussions alive. Meanwhile, Korean senior management, suddenly looped into minor details, felt blindsided that their junior staff hadn't pre-briefed them more thoroughly.

Momentum stalled. The deal nearly collapsed. It was saved only when the CEO flew from the US to Seoul, signaling respect for Korea's hierarchical norms and restoring the trust needed to move forward.

DECISION-MAKING MODES ARE THE HARSHEST BARRIERS

There is the typical US executive known for making quick, actionable decisions "cowboy-style." There is the Brazilian executive known for seeking consensus-driven outcomes. There is the Korean executive known for analyzing and building agreement step by step. And so a negotiation involving all three can be a messy affair. As the Brazilian recalls it:

"On day one, we agreed on three points. On day two, the US–Brazilian team wanted to leapfrog to point four. The Koreans wanted to revisit points one through three. My boss practically had a heart attack."

What looks like hesitation to one side can feel like recklessness to the other. Success in these cross-cultural moments comes from giving each group room to operate in its comfort zone while creating a shared rhythm for decision-making.

For US executives, that may mean keeping an impatient senior leader out of the room so the process can unfold without pressure. For more deliberative cultures, it may mean spelling out the scope, assumptions, and stakes up front so they can contribute with confidence and clarity.

HOW THE BEST TEAMS OVERCOME THESE BARRIERS

Over decades of observation, I've seen these barriers crossed through a four-part escalation of behaviors …

- **Adaptation.** Acknowledging the cultural gaps and working around them, creatively finding a way to merge differing norms.
- **Structural intervention.** Changing the team itself, reconfiguring assignments, or breaking into subgroups to improve collaboration.
- **Managerial intervention.** Resetting the norms of the group and, when necessary, bringing in higher-level leadership to arbitrate.
- **Exit.** The last resort, removing a team member when other approaches have failed.

The key to success with each of these four problem-fixes is early recognition and action. Managers who intervene early and set clear norms, teams that structure interactions to engage everyone, and teams that can see challenges as cultural rather than personal all succeed more often—and with good humor and creativity.

Try Adaptation First

A US software engineer working in Ireland with an Israeli account management team felt slapped by the "in-your-face" decision-making approach he was seeing. It stressed him enough to distract him, and his work suffered. At least until he imposed some structure to preserve his own style while accepting theirs. He realized the confrontations weren't personal; they were cultural. With this reframing, collaboration improved.

Common Cultural Pitfalls in Integrations

Even the best-laid plans can derail without attention to the subtleties. Red flags:

- **Assuming assimilation works.** Expecting the acquired team to instantly adopt the parent company's culture leads to resentment.
- **Underestimating local context.** Ignoring historical practices, community expectations, or tacit knowledge destroys value.
- **Delayed communication.** Waiting too long to share updates fuels rumors and disengagement.
- **Overlooking feedback styles.** Misreading direct versus indirect communication sparks unnecessary conflict.
- **Neglecting multicultural translation.** Failing to bridge global efficiency with local authenticity creates friction, inefficiency, and lost talent.

Cultural alignment is not a nice-to-have. It's a core driver of deal success. Avoid these pitfalls to build the morale that escalates value creation.

Structural Interventions Can Also Work Wonders

A European investment research manager was given a big project with a team representing seven nations. But even after just one day together, she could see that people were associating solely with their own tribes. So she divided the teams into smaller, mixed-culture groups to break down the communication barriers that were evident. Later on, she also brought in a consultant to facilitate meetings when hierarchical tensions tended to silence participation. These structural adjustments helped bubble up keen research ideas that would otherwise have remained hidden.

Managerial Intervention Is Sometimes Necessary

A Canadian refinery safety expert was trying to navigate a complex project in China, and running into roadblocks that he didn't understand. He asked his Chinese counterparts to bring in their superiors to lend insights to the project. By respecting hierarchy and demonstrating his good intentions, he was ultimately able to resolve a number of critical safety issues that might otherwise have gone unnoticed.

Exit Should Remain the Action of Last Resort

With most teams, especially manufacturing teams on steady production schedules, the removal of any personnel is going to create disruption and probably morale issues. So there ought to be very clear missteps, along with mounting tensions on the team, before removal is considered.

Across all four approaches to overcoming barriers, the goal is the same: Leverage the company's cultural capital to create value rather than let misunderstandings sabotage it.

And so with this brief cultural orientation, we can move on to tactics: the playbook for actually putting these insights into practice.

Framing the Postmerger Integration

Merging two companies can be like orchestrating a dance between a ballroom specialist and someone who thinks they're in a mosh pit. This is, of course, two cultures clashing. But if, as the acquisition leader, you set a goal of understanding how the other party in the merger talks, decides, gives feedback, and builds trust, you are no longer flying blind. If your counterpart does the same, then together, you will see the potholes before you hit them, you will line up your teams ably, and you will turn the integration into the value-generating engine you desire rather than the chaotic scramble so widely feared and sadly realized.

At the heart of every successful postmerger integration is a clear understanding of organizational behavior—how people work, communicate, and connect. Once you learn to readily recognize these human patterns, you can transform what seems like cultural chaos into operational harmony.

UNDERSTANDING ORGANIZATIONAL BEHAVIOR

Every company I've ever been involved with communicates in its own unique way. Some are high context, in which history and subtle cues mean everything; a pause, a glance, or a half-smile can speak volumes. Others are low context, in which the principles prefer clarity, explicit instructions, and memos that leave nothing to guesswork.

The integration playbook will reflect these intrinsic patterns. High-context cultures respond to face-to-face meetings, coffee room chatter, and gestures that build rapport. Low-context teams thrive on dashboards, emails, and step-by-step instructions. Ignore the value of either of these, and your messaging won't hit home.

Quick Wins in the First Ninety Days

Momentum matters. *Early actions* signal progress toward meeting the long-term integration strategy. *Early wins* create confidence that there will be success and imprint that confidence—both to internal audiences and external stakeholders. These are:

- **Visible leadership engagement.** Walk the floors, meet teams, personally acknowledge contributions.
- **Early operational wins.** Streamline reporting, implement consistent approval limits, solve a small but high-impact operational pain point.
- **Celebrate small victories.** Pop the bubbly when teams complete key integration milestones.
- **Customer communication.** Announce changes transparently to reassure clients and partners that service quality remains high.
- **Key talent retention.** Identify and engage high-impact employees immediately. Small gestures toward top talent can pay huge dividends short- and long-term.

INFORMATION FLOWS: SAYING IT WITHOUT BREAKING IT

People process information differently. Some need the theory first—the principles, context, and why it matters. Others jump straight into the practical: Give them the what and how, and let results follow. Decision-making mirrors this: Consensus-driven teams chew over every choice, while top-down cultures expect quick, decisive action. Set clear expectations for who decides what—and when—to minimize friction.

Some organizations wear directness like a badge of honor with critiques that are candid, public, and even theatrical. Others soften the edges, delivering criticism privately, almost like passing notes in class. During integration, having a recognized and agreed-upon protocol for feedback is like having a good coxswain in the boat—preventing miscues and misunderstandings and keeping the entire crew rowing in the same direction.

TRUST STRUCTURES: THE ART IS IN THE MELDING

Egalitarian companies are flat planes: Anyone can speak up, and trust is earned through performance. Hierarchical companies flow vertically, where authority and respect are trusted to guide decisions. Task-based cultures build trust through competence. Relationship-based cultures build trust through personal connections. A successful integration respectfully melds these trust structures and human connections into something new—that actually sticks.

CONFLICT AND TIME: HANDLING THE BUMPS

Some companies thrive on open confrontation; others finesse disagreements quietly. Some operate linearly, with sequential projects and hard deadlines; others adjust flexibly as conditions change. Integration plans must set the rules of engagement so that when the bumps come—as they invariably will—there are systems to handle conflict in a timely way.

- What counts as a hard deadline?
- Which disagreements can be aired publicly?
- When is flexibility allowed?

With preset answers to critical operational questions like these, the basic company structure can flex with the conflicts, and the team can gain confidence rather than feel trapped.

Leaders = Multicultural Translators

Company leaders are the linchpins of any successful multicultural integration, acting as translators between cultures and balancing global objectives with local realities.

- **Map leadership styles.** Understand whether managers prefer consensus, command, or a hybrid. Tailor communications accordingly.
- **Bridge task-based trust versus relationships.** Know when to lead with competence and when to invest in relationships.
- **Clarify decision rights.** Who decides what, and at what level? Avoid confusion, codify roles early.
- **Encourage cultural fluency.** Train leaders to read subtle cues, navigate local norms, and communicate strategy across contexts.
- **Model integration behaviors.** Set the tone by visibly adopting the new nested culture's norms, signaling their importance.

By translating effectively, leaders reduce friction, retain talent longer, and accelerate the capture of those all-important synergies.

Outlining the Cultural Integration Plan

Once a deal is announced, the newly joined teams will be looking to see who the new leaders will be and what the plan is. At this critical point in time, you want to know and be able to communicate each of the steps forward that you're hoping the team will take together in the coming months.

There are all kinds of integration checklists you can readily download and use in your integration. They are plentiful and mostly solid. So we are focusing here mostly on the cultural component. As you know by now, that's the harder component, and our running thesis throughout this book. With that caveat out of the way, here is a model blueprint for a powerful cultural alignment and integration in the first 90–180 days and beyond.

CREATE A UNIFIED CULTURAL VISION

The merged company must articulate values that honor the legacy culture while defining a forward-looking identity. These values become the compass guiding decision-making, behaviors, and operational priorities.

COMMUNICATE WITH TRANSPARENCY

Trust is fragile postmerger. Employees and partners alike crave clarity. What's changing? Why? What does it mean for them? They want to know. Overcommunicate the answers to these questions. Acknowledge the concerns your teams have and speak thoughtfully to them about these concerns. The goal here is an important one: to minimize resistance *before* it has a chance to take root and grow into an unsolvable problem.

INTEGRATE AS TACTFULLY AS POSSIBLE

In facing an integration challenge, you know you want to preserve the strengths of both cultures, remove the obvious potential for friction, and create a hybrid culture that accelerates performance. That's the goal, anyway—and if approached wrong, there is so much value that can be lost; but if approached right, so much value can be created.

An easy first step is to identify the elements in each culture that are most easily blended, and figure out how they'll best blend. If an agile start-up may need to merge with a hierarchical legacy company, for instance, what parts of this oil and water blending will go the smoothest?

A harder first step is to figure out right off what the decision-making rights will be, how the governance structures will work, and what the reporting protocols will be.

Whichever of these first steps is taken first, they are best taken, ideally, with a veteran of multiple integrations at your side. There is no substitute for experience in an integration where breaking things is the MO, and breaking them right is no picnic (some say integrations are harder than building a company in the first place). However you approach it—with an experienced hand at your side or alone—plan on focusing on five operational initiatives to demonstrate to the troops the engine is squarely on the tracks and steaming forward. These are ...

1. **Financial reporting.** Create weekly flashes, monthly full reports, and quarterly reviews (to let the merged teams know they are being monitored *and* appreciated).
2. **Approval limits.** Adjust authority thresholds and escalation paths as desired (to set a uniformly high standard of accountability).

3. **Early wins.** Select and pursue projects sure to succeed in the first 90–180 days (to build momentum internally and externally, as well).
4. **Key talent retention.** Proactively engage high-impact employees (to avoid as much attrition as possible).
5. **Customer and partner communication.** Knowing that silence only breeds uncertainty, offer up steady, clear messaging (to recast and harden the cement of trust).

INVOLVE EMPLOYEES WILLINGLY

The goal is to treat integration not as something done to employees but as something built with them. That idea can make some leaders uneasy. Participation, after all, sounds messy. It risks dissent, delay, and even resistance. But the greater risk lies in forcing compliance without commitment.

When employees are invited—genuinely invited—into the integration process, they are far more likely to engage with it. Structured forums such as focus groups, workshops, and informal cultural gatherings give people space to be heard. They can talk about what worked in the old organization, what they valued, what they fear losing, and what they see as promising in the new one.

These conversations do more than surface concerns; they accelerate alignment. Employees begin to process the changes out loud, together. They move from observing the integration to owning it. Over time, the changes stop feeling imposed and start feeling internalized, as people naturally orient themselves around the shared values and direction of the new organization.

OVERCOMMUNICATE STRATEGY

Reassert the vision relentlessly. Clear, consistent messaging prevents drift and anxieties from escalating, and it keeps the organization aligned and purposeful. Reassert that vision again and again. Because just when you get tired of hearing yourself say it, chances are your organization is only just beginning to absorb it.

David Ogilvy, the legendary advertising executive, used to remind his clients that by the time they were sick of seeing an ad campaign, the audience was only encountering it for the first time. That insight has been borne out repeatedly in marketing research: Consumers typically need to hear a message seven or more times before it truly registers and influences behavior.

MONITOR AND ADAPT

Cultural integration is not a single project but a project that requires singular attention over time. This means …

- **Tracking metrics.** Regularly and consistently monitoring employee productivity and engagement.
- **Providing leadership training.** Constantly re-equipping your leadership team to manage ambiguities that arise, build trust structures whenever they see an opening, and address cultural frictions that tend to ebb and flow over time.
- **Conducting reviews.** At six months, twelve months, and eighteen months, typically, review progress against objectives and review the scorecard to call out the successes and the remaining value gaps, as well, allowing you to chart course corrections into the two-year and three-year periods.

JUST KEEP TRANSLATING

At Manitex, and earlier at H-E Parts, we acquired companies ranging from twenty-two to eighty years old. Rushing to overhaul these legacy brands or systems would have met resistance and slowed progress. Instead, we first paid sincere respect to their history. That simple act opened minds: Employees realized they weren't losing anything—they were gaining. And that mindset became a powerful multiplier.

Postmerger integration, in our experience, is less about reports, KPIs, and dashboards and more about people, patterns, and purpose. When we invested in getting the people part right, profits followed naturally. Culture became a measurable asset.

My recommendation? Translate first. Assimilate last. Do it right, and the potential minefield that is multicultural M&A becomes a value-generating engine capable of driving growth, innovation, and lasting competitive advantage.

CONCLUSION

Across these pages, we've shared a set of hard-earned lessons from the field—lessons about growing companies not by scale or brute force alone but by aligning global ambitions with local realities. Again and again, the evidence has pointed in the same direction: Enduring value is created not where strategy overwhelms culture, but where it learns to move with it.

This is the framework I've called the **G.A.L.E. Force—*Global Aim, Local Execution.*** It is not theory. It is a practical response to the real-world complexity of modern business and modern M&A.

When we were building H-E Parts through multiple acquisitions into a global heavy-equipment platform, it became clear that our success would depend far less on financial engineering than on cultural respect, understanding local markets, empowering local leaders, and building global systems that amplified local strengths instead of erasing them. That—more than any spreadsheet—was the work. And that approach transformed a scrappy company into a global platform attractive enough to be acquired itself.

We've also examined the M&A environment as it exists today. A massive generational transfer of businesses is underway as Baby Boomers retire. Lower-middle-market deals are proving to be among the most compelling opportunities available. Private equity and sovereign capital are abundant. And globalization—once assumed to flatten differences—has revealed the opposite truth: The more connected the world becomes, the more local culture matters.

This paradox is why the **G.A.L.E. Force** framework has become so powerful. Global reach now amplifies local identity. And the organizations that win are not always those with the deepest pockets, but those with the deepest cultural intelligence.

While the global markets are fast evolving, there are some constants in business—especially in an M&A context. Sellers are regularly underestimating what it takes to exit well. Buyers are still overestimating the power of strategy and capital alone. And even seasoned dealmakers are discovering that yesterday's playbooks fall short in a world where psychology, identity, and local norms increasingly determine outcomes.

Given both these changes and constants, we've looked at how companies can best align strategy, culture, and leadership so that M&A deals don't just close satisfactorily, but yield handsome payouts and multiples.

We've seen that value creation is now the high art of **alignment**—strategy with culture, leadership with incentives, systems with human behavior. When that alignment is achieved, deals don't just close; they compound. Arithmetic becomes exponential.

Culture, whether leaders acknowledge it or not, is now the terrain of business. Every place—Santiago, Perth, Billings—wakes with its own rhythm, rituals, and expectations. These are immovable facts. I learned that lesson early in Chile when strategic meetings were interrupted by a national soccer match. I had a choice: Resist reality and fail quietly, or leverage it. By choosing the latter—by weaving local passion into the company's fabric—we doubled the business in four years.

The lesson was simple but profound: Success across borders requires translation, not assimilation. The best acquirers become cultural interpreters. They give teams room to operate in their own rhythm while moving together toward a shared aim and ambition. Authenticity replaces uniformity. Culture moves from the brake pedal to the accelerator.

At H-E Parts, we codified this into **PRACTISE**—a values-driven gearbox built for heavy industry and multicultural complexity. Perseverance. Responsiveness. Accountability. Communication. Teachability. Innovation. Safety. Excellence. These weren't slogans. They were operational tools that guided decisions, aligned teams, and accelerated integration.

Leadership matters deeply—but not in the superhero sense. Sustainable performance comes from clarity, engagement, and measurement. It comes from leaders who build teams, embed values, align incentives, and design systems that endure beyond them.

To identify those leaders, I developed **DRiiVE**—Drive, Restraint, Intelligence, Innovation, Virtue, and team-centered Ego. Leaders who embody these traits don't wear capes. Their superpower is collaboration. And in today's environment, that is the trait that scales.

When it comes to exits, the message is clear: Preparation is everything. Successful sales are not lucky; they are disciplined. Especially in family-owned businesses, the financial outcome and the legacy outcome are inseparable. The best exits come from companies built to thrive without their founders—companies with clarity, clean systems, aligned leadership, and a story that reflects their true value.

We saw this at Manitex when our preparation and alignment ahead of the Tadano acquisition unlocked value that would otherwise have remained hidden. Strategy, talent, process, and culture were aligned. One plus one became six.

And That Brings Us to Today

After negotiating the Manitex transaction, I faced a familiar question: What next?

Another operating role was an option. But so was something more impactful—helping others navigate the journey ahead. Not through abstract consulting, but through applied experience. That idea became ***Resurgence Advisory***.

In the years since, my partners and I have worked on more than fifty transactions, bringing large-company rigor to lower-middle-market deals and treating postmerger integration as the engine of value creation—not an afterthought.

We are operators helping operators. We know what it takes to build value, unlock it, and realize it.

If this book has helped you better understand the terrain ahead—if it has helped you trim your sails, read the winds, and move with confidence into open water—then it has done its job. The journey is yours. The forces are real. And when aligned, they are powerful.

Global aim.

Local execution.

And the courage to run both well.

To learn more, visit www.JMichaelCoffey.com.

ACKNOWLEDGMENTS

To Sherrie—my wife and best friend for more than thirty years. Thank you for enduring the rigor of an international career, which all too often followed me into weekends, holidays, and family vacations. You have been my foundation, encouraging me to reach for higher goals, and my constant comfort during moments of uncertainty and self-doubt. None of this would have been possible without your unwavering love, patience, and belief in me.

I would also like to acknowledge the leaders and employees of two organizations that played defining roles in my professional journey: H-E Parts International (HEPI) and Manitex International. My experiences with you challenged and shaped my understanding of what it means to lead a multinational enterprise amid complexity, uncertainty, and constant change.

G.A.L.E. Force is the culmination of lessons learned alongside remarkable colleagues and peers. I am especially grateful to the executive teams at both companies. While the stories shared here may give the impression of unbroken success, the reality is far more nuanced. Failure, missteps, and shortcomings were frequent teachers, and I am deeply thankful to the colleagues who helped transform those moments into learning and future success.

At H-E Parts International, I owe a special debt of gratitude to Steve McBrayer, former CFO and CEO. During a period marked by both a global financial crisis and the inherent fragility of a young enterprise, Steve's judgment, resolve, and steadiness were instrumental to the company's survival and growth. His timely feedback, thoughtful coaching, and uncanny sense of humor left a lasting imprint on both the organization and on me personally. Much of the insight reflected in this book can be traced back to those refining conversations over morning coffee with Steve.

To David Langevin, Chairman of Manitex International and its founder from 2003, for his persistence, dedication, and steady hand.

To my parents, thank you for your love and faithfulness. I am especially grateful to my mother, Carol, whose perseverance and grit—so often required of single mothers—shaped my understanding of resilience. Her example continues to guide me.

I would also like to thank Jim Recer, a close friend and trusted confidant, who served as a steady sounding board as I navigated the challenges and responsibilities of business leadership. His perspective, honesty, and unwavering support were invaluable.

To Charles Snyder and Bill Traylor, mentors during my time at American Equipment (AMECO), thank you for setting in motion both my path into this industry and my enduring passion for it.

I am also grateful to H-E Parts' financial sponsors, Frontenac and Champ Venture, for their uncommon support and timely challenges. In particular, Paul Carbery, Mike Langdon, and Gareth Banks—thank you for traveling the world and going far beyond the boardroom to work alongside the leadership team in the trenches.

Finally, while this book is not religious in nature, I acknowledge the faith that undergirds my life and work. For nearly forty years, my Christian faith has shaped the values I hold most dear and has sustained me through moments when I have fallen short of them. Christ has been both my North Star and my compass in life and in business.

ABOUT THE AUTHOR

J. MICHAEL COFFEY is known for bringing innovative solutions to industrial businesses. Coffey is a seasoned executive and strategic advisor with thirty years of experience leading industrial, manufacturing, and value-added distribution companies. He retired as CEO of Manitex International (NASDAQ: MNTX) following a successful take-private sale of the global mobile crane and aerial work platform manufacturer to Tadano Ltd. Previously, he served as CEO and COO of private equity-backed H-E Parts International, a mining services company with thirty remanufacturing and distribution centers across seven countries, which was sold to Hitachi Construction Equipment in 2016.

Coffey has extensive experience guiding global, multicultural enterprises through merger and acquisition growth. These experiences were formative in helping Coffey bridge gaps between M&A strategy and value. In 2022, he led the turnaround of Manitex International (NASDAQ: MNTX), launching the three-year **Elevating Excellence** strategic road map, which delivered 30 percent growth and a 400 percent improvement in EBITDA.

He holds an MBA from Goizueta Business School, Emory University, and resides in Atlanta with his wife of thirty years. Together, they celebrate being the parents of two adult daughters.

ABOUT THE AUTHOR

www.ingramcontent.com/pod-product-compliance
Lightning Source LLC
Chambersburg PA
CBHW020544130726
48054CB00019B/48

* 9 7 9 8 8 9 7 0 1 0 6 9 1 *